Using Imagery
in
Creative Problem Solving

by
Michael T. Bagley, Ph.D.

Second Printing

Trillium Press
Unionville, New York
Toronto, Ontario

Trillium Press
First Avenue
Unionville, NY 10988
(914) 726-4444
FAX: (914) 726-3824

Trillium Press
203 College St
Suite 200
Toronto, Ontario
M5T 1P9 Canada

ISBN: 0-89824-104-9

Printed in the United States of America by the Royal Fireworks Press of Unionville, New York.

TABLE OF CONTENTS

Chapter   TITLE   Page

1   IMAGERY: A NATURAL HUMAN ABILITY 1
2   MIND AND HUMAN POTENTIAL 9
3   IMAGE CREATION AND PROBLEM SOLVING 22
4   CPS-IMAGERY EXERCISES 46
Bibliography 109

Introduction

"Imagination is not a talent of some people; it is the health of
every individual."
                              Ralph Waldo Emerson

Imagery is one of the terms most associated with the mid-1980's.
Despite the proliferation and acclaim, most Americans remain un-
aware of its true nature and application to life. Never before has a
society thirsted so for imagination in movies, in literature. What is
it about imagination, that has captured the minds and hearts of so
many, with such tenaciousness?

    While this text doesn't provide a definitive answer to this question,
it does however, clearly demonstrate why imagery is so awesome!
There is something special about imagery. It's difficult to describe,
one must truly experience it fully to understand its magnitude and
infiniteness.

    The title, *Using Imagery In Creative Problem Solving*, was chosen
because it best describes the active and creative nature of the image
process. Imagery is a highly creative act—perhaps our most creative
human function. It is sheer magic! Its application and effect on
learning and living is tremendous.

    Until now, most of the imagery work in education has centered
around Guided Fantasy Imagery and more recently Guided
Academic Imagery. This text represents a bold shift in the study
and use of imagery. It clearly demonstrates the importance of Non-
Guided Imagery (images evoked and controlled by the imager). It
makes that necessary link between learning the skill of imagery and
using imagery successfully in everyday life.

    The basic theme of the text is Imagery in Creative Problem Sol-
ving. No one needs to be reminded that the problems facing society
are becoming more complex each day. None of us can avoid prob-

lems, as they are an integral part of living. However, successful living depends greatly on how one approaches problems. The "mind set" or attitude one has toward dealing with problems is crucial to productive living. It is the development of a positive mind set that interests me most, and is the major force behind *Using Imagery In Creative Problem Solving*. I want young people to not feel defeated by each and every problem that comes along. Instead, I want these young people to approach problems in a "positive," . . . "I'm going to find a solution attitude," which I hope they will carry with them into adulthood.

Using Imagery In Creative Problem Solving provides a framework, it is a vehicle one can use to attack problems more creatively. Too often we look at problems from a narrow, linear perspective, looking at the same set of variables and circumstances over and over again. Using creative imagery allows one to take a fresh, new and different view of the problem, which ultimately can lead to very interesting and productive idea finding.

The basic purpose of the text is to:

a)   expand one's knowledge and understanding of the potential of imagery,
b)   provide a framework for attacking problems more creatively,
c)   promote greater use of non-guided imagery,
d)   foster a more positive "mind set" toward encountering and solving problems.

The text is written in an important progression, taking the reader through a series of creativity and imagery principles. In Chapter 1, the reader will find a discussion on the importance of creativity and the creative process. In Chapter 2, the reader will explore some new issues and trends relating to the potential of mind and consciousness. Chapter 3 outlines the step-by-step approach used in solving problems through imagery. Chapter 4 contains Creative Problem Solving Exercises each with activity options and suggestions for creative writing assignments. At the end of the book, the reader will find a select reference list on imagery and related areas and a list of Music To Image By.

CHAPTER ONE

Imagery:
A Natural Human Ability

> "Before the dawn of history men were vividly imaging goals essential to their survival and reinforcing those images by painting them with primitive but lasting colors on the ceilings or walls of the caves that were their homes."
>
> Anonymous

Before words, images were. The human brain programs and self-programs through its images. The human mind is a slide projector with an infinite number of slides stored in its library, an instant retrieval system and an endlessly cross-referenced subject catalog. Imagery is the way we think. Building a model, driving a car, learning a game, fixing a bike, playing a sport—all skills are acquired through the image-making process. Imagery is the ultimate consciousness tool.

Albert Einstein has said he discovered the theory of relativity by picturing (imaging) himself riding on a ray of light. He has written that words did not play a role in his thought. "The psychical elements in thought are certain signs and more or less clear images which can be voluntarily reproduced and combined."

During our lifetime most of us will spend about four years involved in actual image production, through dreams, daydreams and directed imagery. It is a normal human function of the brain to produce visual images. Most of the time we aren't even aware that such a process is going on in our heads. We have become so overly dependent on, and preoccupied with words that we have forgotten about our innate capacity to create pictures. The most powerful vehicle for change is the image; it is the central, pivotal part of mind.

A BRIEF HISTORY OF IMAGERY

The earliest record of visualization experiences is in the form of pictures, visual images. During the Ice Age—60,000 to 10,000 B.C.—cave dwellers in France, Spain, Africa and Scandanavia painted on the walls of their caves representations of the images that they saw. Most of these paintings are of animals that people hunted. The use of imagery techniques for physical healing dates back well before the rise of experimental science. In fact, imagery may be the most ancient healing technique used by primitive man. The earliest records of such techniques are found on cuneiform slabs from Babylonia and Summaria. Even today, Indian tribes such as the Canadian Eskimo and the Navahos of the American Southwest use forms of healing based on visualizations.

In psychology, hypnosis is one of the oldest techniques to use imagery. It was through hypnosis that psychologists first discovered memory images. Many of the imagery techniques being used in hospitals and clinics today have their origin from these ancient practices.

In the last hundred years, specialists in different fields have begun to rediscover the existence and meaning of imagery. Historians, religious scholars, archaeologists, physicians, psychologists, and educators have begun to study the nature of the inner image as it relates to their area of specialization.

The image is as old as man himself—what modern man is doing, is recreating a passionate relationship with nature.

THE IMPORTANCE OF CREATIVITY

"My feeling is that the concept of creativeness and the concept of the healthy, self-actualizing fully human person seem to be coming closer and closer together, and may, perhaps, turn out to be the same thing."

Abraham H. Maslow

The more one creates the better one feels about self—the better one feels about self, the more one creates. As we begin this journey into the world of creativity, imagination and imagery, I would like you to keep this so-called "health concept" of creativity in mind. As Ralph Waldo

Emerson said, "Imagination is not a talent of some people but the health of every person." Nothing has been more rewarding to me than to watch the excitement, joy, and positive feeling expressed by students during creative work. I've seen this love on the face of a five year old experiencing a guided fantasy through a magical candy land and the same love on the faces of elders involved in creative dramatics. The appreciation and benefits of creativity is universal. I don't believe that there exists any discipline or subject more important to an individual than creativity. The encouragement of creative thinking would seem to be the most necessary and immediate goal of all concerned people. Yet, too few are interested in pursuing the study and application of creativity into their professional and personal lives.

> "In a time when knowledge, constructive and destructive, is advancing by the most incredible leaps and bounds into a fantastic atomic age, genuinely creative adaptation seems to represent the only possibility that man can keep abreast of the kaleidoscopic change in his world. With scientific discovery and invention proceeding, we are told, at the rate of geometric progression, a generally passive and culture bound people cannot cope with the multiplying issues and problems. Unless individuals, groups, and nations can imagine, construct, and creatively revise new ways of relating to these complex changes, the lights will go out. Unless man can make new and original adaptations to his environment as rapidly as his science can change the environment, culture will perish. Not only individual maladjustment and group tensions, but international annihilation will be the price we pay for a lack of creativity."
>
> Carl P. Rogers

As Carl Sagan states "mere critical thinking, without the search for new patterns, is sterile and doomed. To solve complex problems in changing circumstances requires the activity of both cerebral hemispheres." (Sagan, 1977). The physicist, Capra (1975) argues that rational knowing is useless if not accompanied and enhanced by intuitive knowing. He equates intuition with new creative insights. Even more provocative is a statement by historian Arnold Toynbee (1964), "to give a fair chance to potential creativity is a matter of life and death for any society." Toynbee adds a final challenge to our nation by saying that "America's manifest destiny in the next chapter of history is to help the indigent majority of mankind to struggle upward towards a better life than it has ever dreamed in the past." And if she is to embark successfully upon this mission, he concludes that "America must treasure and foster all the creative ability that she has in her."

TOWARD A DEFINITION OF CREATIVITY

One of the misconceptions about creativity is that it is a skill possessed by a certain few. This is absolutely incorrect. This type of thinking is the result of conceptualizing creativity only as a work of great artistic talent, e.g., a beautiful painting, a sculpture, etc. Not so—creativity is all around us in our everyday actions and thoughts. We experience creativity when we dress, cook, or daydream. It is so much a part of our lives and we don't even realize its full extent.

If you read the literature on creativity, you will find numerous definitions. Some very specific, others extremely verbose. Anything powerful and all encompassing is usually difficult to define, a la love! One way of viewing creativity is to consider it as the association of thoughts, facts, ideas, etc., into a new and relevant configuration. Parnes (1977) considers creativity as "a function of knowledge, imagination, and evaluation." He goes on to say, "that we might consider creativity as a kaleidoscope: needless to say, the more pieces we have in the drum, the more possible patterns we can produce." Likewise, in creative learning, the greater our knowledge, the more patterns, combinations, or ideas we can achieve. Often I ask my students to look at an illustration or a painting and identify the features or entities that are known, i.e., aspects of the picture or image that we are familiar with; then I ask them to describe what made the picture or image creative. How were the known entities arranged or associated to form a new original pattern, idea, or creation? For instance, in the mystical vision of William Blake's painting, *The Ancient Days*, I might ask my students to identify the known entities. In this case, they might identify sky, man, long hair, beard, etc. What makes the picture representative of the creative act is that a man, unclothed, is centered within the sun, reaching out and touching the top of a mountain. It is the arrangement, the association of known entities into new patterns which gives the picture its creative tone. A very functional definition offered by Barbara Clark (1979) is called the integrative definition of creativity. Clark's definition has four major components; they are:

4

THINKING:	this is the cognitive, thought producing, brainstorming approach toward generating original ideas
SENSING:	this is the concrete, product, artistic sensing that one would use during the origination of a work as art
FEELING:	the feeling component is the emotional, affective somatic response that one experiences during the creative process and fourth,
INTUITION:	the imaginary, subconscious, visionary impulse or image received by the person during the creative process.

The important concept here is that while some theorists allude to one component in their definition statement of creativity, most will discuss creativity in terms of Clark's four components. Each of these four components may be present during the creative act. Some are more intense and recognizable than others, but all are present to some extent. Clark's paradigm provides us a structure for developing curriculum in the area of creativity. I will discuss this point later as we go into methodologies.

THE CREATIVE PROCESS

Dr. G. Wallis (1936) theorized that the creative process consists of four stages. The four stages Wallis describes are based on the accounts of famous peoples' creative experiences. The first stage is PREPARATION. In this stage, people gather the information, data, tools and materials that seem applicable to the problem they are working on. The second stage is called INCUBATION. This is a time when we may or may not release our conscious hold on the problem. During incubation we might rest, relax or turn our attention in another direction. During this so-called associative stage, the unconscious is active, constantly shifting and realigning itself. Most theorists believe incubation is the most critical stage in creativity. The third stage Wallis calls ILLUMINATION. This is when the "aha!" — the solution — spontaneously jumps into consciousness, often at an unexpected moment (perhaps during our best incubation period) and is visually accompanied by feelings of certainty and joy. I love to sit just outside the seminar room during a creativity course and wait in anticipation for the shouts of joy, usually in the form of screams, as students light up with a new idea or solution to a problem. The final stage in Wallis's model is VERIFICATION. In this stage people begin to test the validity of their ideas or work, and do it through organizing data and conducting experiments. It is this stage that Parnes (1977)

5

refers to as the concept of the "Dynamic/Delicate Balance." He states, "The dynamic balance of the full creative process seems to involve the balance between the judgement and the imagination: between the open awareness of the environment through all the senses and the deep self-searching into layer upon layer of data stored in the memory; between the logic and the emotion; between the processes of making it happen and those of letting it happen; between the insights and the actions."

Dr. Sidney Parnes of the Creative Studies Program, State University of Buffalo, site of the infamous Creative Problem Solving, Institute describes the creative process according to the following diagram:

| SENSORY | ASSOCIATION | INTERRELATIONSHIP | CREATIVE |
| IMPRESSIONS | PROCESS | FORMED | EXPRESSION |

During the sensory impression stage, a person is exposed to various stimuli (sounds, lights, textures, etc.) and is encouraged to be open and free (Parnes tells his audience to remove their brakes). The second stage association process, similar to incubation, is when the unconscious mind is shaking up all the pieces, mixing, sorting, etc., i.e., looking at all possibilities and combinations before jolting the information to the conscious mind. When that does occur, we move into the next stage which is the forming of interrelationships. It is here that the aha! or new idea is formed. Following the new configuration is some form of creative expression—a vehicle to deliver the new thought, idea or action to the external world.

According to mind researcher Dr. Elmer Green (1977) "truly creative thinking takes place when the mind is in a state of inner calm. In other words the great and creative discoveries in science, in the arts and in the corporate office generally come at times when the mind is at peace with itself."

It has been documented that creative people often are very aware of specific physical conditions or actions during which they get their ideas. Mozart commented that his ideas often came while riding in a carriage or walking after a good meal. M. Samuels, (1975) lists some conditions most frequently cited by creative people. They include the following: riding in a car, train, or airplane, walking at leisure, bathing, reading, watching television, listening to music, napping, walking in the middle of the night, dreaming, gazing or staring at an object. The basic mind-stilling and relaxed attention fostered by such activities corresponds with the non-ordinary states of mind conducive for creative illumination. I will discuss mind states in more detail in Chapter 2.

The important message, then, is that conditions surrounding creative effort, the conditions under which people incubate and illuminate best, can be consciously created, reproduced, and controlled. Eliot Hutchinson, a Cambridge University researcher, hints about the attitudes that underlie the birth of a creative idea and offers the following:

Increase your motivation by anticipating the satisfaction of achievement.

Increase your preparation by believing the problem is not insoluble for you.

Believe the answer will come although you may have to wait.

Realize that rest is essential when you feel defeated by a problem.

It is important that we discuss the creative process with our students, and describe all the varying conditions, events and thoughts that effect our production of creative ideas. There is so much more "processes" information available to the learner. It is a our role as learning facilitators to make available this valuable knowledge.

In this first chapter, I have presented some basic concepts relating to the study of creativity. This information will serve as a foundation as we begin to explore more sophisticated concepts concerning the human mind.

BLOCKS TO CREATIVITY

It's very difficult to develop your creative potential when parents, school and society demonstrate less than positive support for creative endeavors. Part of the problem stems from ignorance, a lack of awareness as to the importance of creativity in one's life. Another factor is our educational system which greatly emphasizes the development of our logical mind at the expense of our creative mind. More than 90% of our schooling tends to train our judicial faculties. Our imaginative powers initially grow faster than reason, but then tend to wane while reason rises in ascendancy. Unless concerted effort is made to nurture our creative minds, the gap between rational thought and imaginative thought widens, with the former gaining extreme superiority. E. P. Torrance (1975) and others have clearly demonstrated that at age nine, children seem to drop significantly in creative aptitude. Cultural factors such as sex-typing, religious beliefs, social values, occupational choices, are strong influences and have potentially dramatic effect on the attitude one develops to creativity. As these cultural behaviors are modeled and reinforced, emotional attitudes to creativity are developed which can be described as fearful, non-risking, cautious, overly defensive, reserved—all attributes contributing to a negative effect in creative behavior. Despite the fact that human beings have a natural capacity to think in visual images as well as words, our educational system continues to over-emphasize the verbal processes. Jean Houston (1980) states "that many children are natural visualizers (imagers), in fact, many are much more geared to visual thinking than verbal thinking." She goes on to say, "many of these children are cut off from their visualizing (imaging) capacity by the verbal-linear processes that the educational system imposes on them."

Dr. Dale Ironson, a training and development specialist at Stanford University, takes an interesting approach toward the stifling of creativity. In an article entitled, "Human High Technology: Possible Programming Errors," Ironson states: "You would not want to operate your IBM personal computer with a program that was written by a five year old child. Yet, we all do this with our minds and then live by limiting beliefs, assumptions and expectations. Programs written when we were young may be limiting our ability to think creatively." This analogy is very interesting in that we program people at an early age to believe that creativity is for a chosen few, that most people do not possess any creative skills. If we play these negative tapes often enough and long enough there will be no question as to what our behavior will be like. In Chapter 2, the reader will find a more in depth discussion of playing "mind tapes."

MIND AND HUMAN POTENTIAL

"We think much less than what we know. We know much less than what we love. We love much less than what there is, and to this precise extent, we are much less than what we are."

R. D. Laing
The Politics of Experience

The theme for this second chapter relates to a statement made back in the late 1800's by the father of American Psychology, William James, "The greatest discovery of my generation is that human beings, by changing the inner attitude of their minds, can change the outer aspect of their lives. It is too bad that more people will not accept this tremendous discovery and begin living it." I wonder how many more generations must go by before the majority of people begin to truly understand what James is saying, and start living it. We are so filled with non-positive attitudes concerning our abilities and potential that we don't even give ourselves an opportunity to learn about or experience the power of our inner imagination. As Barbara Brown (1980) says in her book, *Supermind*, "For most of man's existence these powers of mind have been shrouded behind ignorance and myths, or held sacred and unknowable by philosophy or assumed to be predictable and trivial by science." Brown, Believes that "Sleeping within everyone is a mind of superior intellect and ability, a mind that modern man preoccupied with the wonders of physical nature, has neglected and virtually silenced—the bulk of scientific authority considers mind a foolish and unwarranted concept." I would like this section of the text to be viewed as your personal "mind stretching" chapter. My aim is to present different points of view regarding the extraordinary potential of the human mind. There are so much data and research available today on human potential that we owe it to ourselves to make these facts and knowledge part of our mental library. In order to appreciate and utilize the imaginative powers within you, it is necessary to understand the dynamics of the mind—only then will we be free enough and open enough to welcome imagination into our lives as a legitimate and useful human tool. So relax and let's explore some of the issues and facts concerning the lesser known dimension of our existence.

MIND AS A MENTAL LIBRARY

Dr. Willer Penfield, a neurosurgeon from Montreal, theorizes that every experience—sight, sound, smell, and taste—registers as a particular pattern in the brain and that this pattern stays on long after the experience is consciously forgotten. Through thousands of experiments with patients, Penfield found that human experience is recorded within our brain cells in the form of image processes which have "amazing original retention." During gentle electrical stimulation on a point in the interpretive cortex of the brain, the patients, who were under local anesthesia and thus conscious at all times, reported pictures which progressed in time and unfolded more details with repeated application of the electrode. These images, which progressed during repeated stimulation, also contained strong sense impressions, such as feelings and thoughts. Patients reported that they were not merely remembering but actually reliving the event of the past as a current experience, while as observers, they were also simultaneously aware of the present. Penfield referred to their imagery evocations as "experimental responses" or "strips of time." Isn't that a fascinating concept—to think that everything we see, touch, feel, taste, sense, is constantly being registered and filed in the storage bank of our mental library. You ask a fifth or sixth grader to write about a flower and s/he says "I have nothing to say" or "I don't know what to say," etc. Isn't that sad! If only that person was aware that within his/her mental library lies perhaps thousands of experiences filed under the category of flower (if you follow Penfield's reasoning, all experiences a child has had with a flower, e.g., touched it, pulled it apart, smelled it, tasted it, saw it in a vase, saw it in a field of flowers, pinned on a person's clothing, heard about it in numerous children's stories, listened to it being discussed by family, friends, teachers, clergy, etc. are filed in that youngster's "bio-computer"). The problem is, most of us do not know how to program our mental machinery so that we can access this information on a command. Don't worry! Later, I will share some ways of tapping this oil well!

In Figure 1, you will observe that I have divided the brain into two common hypothetical divisions, conscious and subconscious. Scientists, say that it is the subconscious mind where our experiences are stored and retrieved. Note the various labels used to describe the subconscious mind. There is a commonality among these descriptions which are used by researchers representing several scientific disciplines, that is they all give you the feeling of infiniteness, and enormous value. The geometric designs represent a hypothetical filing system where all our previous experiences are stored. Some brain researchers say that our filing system contains more than a trillion bytes of data.

BIO-COMPUTER

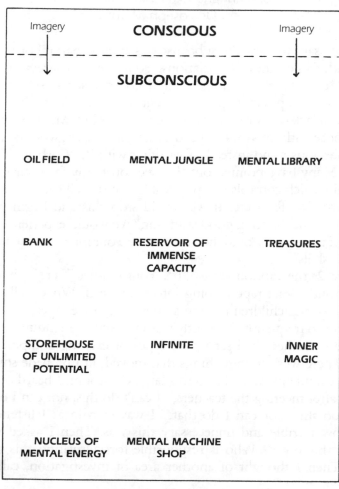

Teach this concept to your students. It will give them a better feeling about self and you'll introduce them to their very own personal "bio-computer." This realization that they possess such vast quantities of data is a first step toward activating their "imagination power." They must believe in their own worth and potential. Using the concept of the mental library as a storehouse of immense capacity should at least get your students to say, "Hey, perhaps there is a lot stored up here!"

TAPPING YOUR SUBCONSCIOUS POWER

"Within your subconscious depths lie infinite wisdom, infinite power, and infinite supply of all that is necessary, which is waiting for development and expression."
Dr. Joseph Murphy

It is not necessary to view the subconscious as supernatural or mystical. If we could forget these associations, some real progress could be achieved. Mention subconscious, altered consciousness, self-hypnosis, mediation and people stop paying attention. They do so because of ignorance and lack of awareness of the nature of mind. Many Americans, especially those with stress and psychosomatic illness, are working against their subconscious mind instead of working with it. "Garbage in—garbage out." Many have pointed out that we constantly feed our subconscious mind (which controls our physical hardware) all sorts of negative thoughts, worries, fears etc. If we would stop this and begin putting 'good stuff in" and "getting good stuff out," we would experience better health and of course we would then begin to use our innate and wonderful imagination skills.

In Figure 2, the caption reads, "It's Your Choice." Truly, it is your choice to decide what tape to plug into your head. What really upsets me is to see young children playing so many negative tapes, and worse, playing them so frequently. I recently was involved in an inquiry learning course where teachers had set up all types of exciting equipment and materials. There were strange things that moved, lit up, made sounds— and then the students walked into this large classroom. I heard one little person say after meeting the teachers, "I can't do this, nor can I do that, nor can I do this, nor can I do that." I was in pain as I listened and thought how terrible and unnecessary this was. Then I asked myself, Where did this begin? Who is responsible for cultivating this type of thinking? Then I thought of another area of investigation, called the

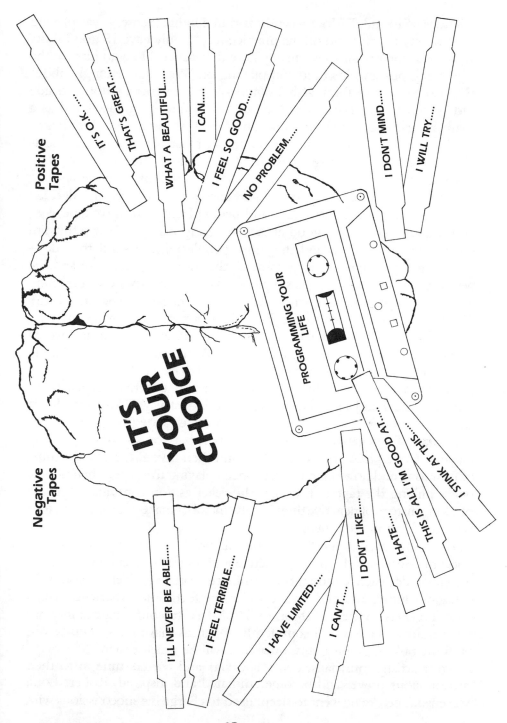

Positive Tapes

IT'S O.K.......
THAT'S GREAT......
WHAT A BEAUTIFUL......
I CAN......
I FEEL SO GOOD......
NO PROBLEM......
I DON'T MIND......
I WILL TRY......

PROGRAMMING YOUR LIFE

IT'S YOUR CHOICE

Negative Tapes

I'LL NEVER BE ABLE......
I FEEL TERRIBLE......
I HAVE LIMITED......
I CAN'T......
I DON'T LIKE......
I HATE......
THIS IS ALL I'M GOOD AT......
I STINK AT THIS......

"Genesis of I Can't." More recently and in a lighter sense, I was playing golf and my partner said on the practice tee, "I only have 15 good shots in me so I don't want to waste any here in practice." I could just see the tape being put into his head and playing on. Well, sure enough, about 15 or so shots into the match I could see my partner's whole attitude and poise change. Tension and a lack of confidence surfaced and as a result his game changed radically. The tape (his inner thoughts) began to dictate his play. A very simple point, yet most of us haven't a clue as to the amount of negative tapes we play and how often we play them. For years I have played a Bagley tape called, "I'm lousy at remembering names." Then one day, (you know—practice what your preach) I decided to stop playing this negative tape and begin playing a positive tape, e.g., "I am going to become good at remembering names." As a result I'm improving each month and the more people tell me—and they do—"you're great at remembering names," the more I concentrate and the better I feel. Yes, it can be as simple as that. An activity I do in training is to have people actually write the title of a negative tape on a blank cassette, then I ask them to begin pulling out and destroying the long tape. They pull and pull and pull and soon the whole room is covered with mounds of tape. People cry, laugh! What emotions! But what an experience—a very powerful one, indeed. I haven't done this activity with children yet, but I think that it will be very effective, especially for fourth graders and up. The cassette tape industry will love me! Stop! Before you continue with the text, get a blank cassette (inexpensive one) and think of a negative tape you play often that you would like to stop playing. Get a piece of tape, entitle it and then if you're alone just think of how long and how often you have been playing this tape. Then slowly, begin pulling the tape out, feeling the relief as you continue to get rid of a long history of negative thinking. Remember make your subconscious your friend, not your enemy.

Your subconscious mind is like the soil which accepts any kind of seed, good or bad. Your thoughts are active and might be likened unto seeds. Negative, destructive thoughts continue to work negatively in your subconscious mind, and in due time will come forth into experience which corresponds with them (J. Murphy 1968). To tap our innate ability, we must think positively and confidently. We must have faith in ourselves; then the task of tapping this inner fuel will be much easier.

Great artists, musicians, poets, speakers and writers tune in to their subconscious power and become animated and inspired. Robert Louis Stevenson, before he went to sleep, used to charge his subconscious with

14

the task of evolving stories for him while he slept. He was accustomed to ask his subconscious to give him a good marketable thriller when his bank account was low. Stevenson said, the intelligence of his deeper mind gave him the story piece by piece, like a serial. Mark Twain confided to the world on many occasions that he never worked in his life. All his humor and all his great writings were due to the fact that he taped the inexhaustible reservoir of his subconscious mind. My favorite example of this phenomenon is the following:

> I shut my eyes for a few minutes with my portable typewriter on my knee. I make my mind a blank and wait and then, as clearly as I would see real children, my characters stand before me in my mind's eye .... The story enacted almost as if I had a private cinema screen there ... I don't know what is going to happen. I am in the happy position of being able to write a story and read it for the first time at one and the same moment .... Sometimes a character makes a joke, a really funny one that makes me laugh as I type it on my paper and I think "Well, I couldn't have thought of that myself in a hundred years !" and then I think: "Well who did think of it?"
>
> (Stone, 1974)
Cinematographic imagery of Enid Blyton relative to the occurrence of her ideas for the Noddy stories.

Murphy (1968) states that over 90 percent of our mental life is subconscious.

SOME SUGGESTIONS FOR TAPPING YOUR SUBCONSCIOUS POWERS

1. Develop belief and faith in the fact that our subconscious mind is a reservoir of knowledge and information.
2. Be sure to speak to your subconscious mind with authority and conviction, and it will conform to your command.
3. Get rid of the negatives—program yourself with positives.
4. Develop an expectancy attitude where you begin to anticipate receiving gifts from your subconscious (these gifts can be in the form of creative ideas).
5. Develop your own method and style for going within. Don't follow

someone else's. Create your own personalized effective stimulus.

6. Don't subject yourself to the skeptical and derogatory criticisms of the unbelieving.
7. Learn effective ways to relax and still your mind—a relaxed mind allows you to focus and concentrate, it is a passage to the inner depths.
8. Become skilled at mental imagery, I believe it is our most valuable human resource. (Chapter 3 and Part 2 of this text is devoted to developing this skill.)

THE USE OF ALTERED STATES OF CONSCIOUSNESS FOR LEARNING AND PROBLEM SOLVING

The use of altered states of consciousness for problem solving, positive programming, mental exploration or relaxation is perfectly safe and can benefit anyone. You are already familiar with altered states, although you may not realize it. You pass through these states at least twice a day, as you awaken in the morning and as you fall asleep at night. Altered states of consciousness have been explained by brain researchers and medical practitioners on the basis of brain-wave activity. This activity has been divided into four levels, based on cycles-per-second of brain activity:

Beta: Full Consciousness
Alpha: Falling asleep at night. Awakening in the morning. Meditation. Imagery.
Theta: Early states of sleep. Deep meditation. Deep imagery.
Delta: Full sleep to deepest sleep.
Alpha, theta, and delta are all considered altered states of consciousness.

How do we know when we are in an altered state of consciousness? Brain-wave patterns are used to measure the amount of activity in the "visual cortex." The electroencephalograph (EEG machine), developed by Hans Bergen in 1924, is the primary means for determining the level of consciousness one is experiencing. These brain wave patterns have no sensory concomitants—that is, there are no sensory processes by which we can detect the presence of brain wave activity. We can detect muscle contractions, cold hands, or a pounding heart, but there is no way to sense brain wave activity (E. Green 1977). What we sense and control is not the brain wave itself, but a state of consciousness.

Barbara Brown's (1974) brain wave research also focused on the kinds of awareness associated with different brain wave patterns.

16

Much of what is known today concerning altered states of consciousness and creativity have come from interviews with (or from documents, journals, biographies, etc.) artists and scientists who had a special awareness of "consciousness shifting," during their incubation and illumination stage of the creative process. Many described a kind of reverie or near-dream state in which intuitive ideas and solutions (in contradistinction to logical problem-solving solutions) come to consciousness in the form of creative images. Here are some accounts of famous people who used altered states and imagery in the creative process.

William Blake, John Milton, and Samuel Coleridge are classic examples of artists and poets who received inspiration through imagery while in unusual states of consciousness.

Jean Cocteau (1952) wrote to his friend Jacques Maritain, "The poet is at the disposal of his night. He must clean his house and await its visualization." He explained, "The play that I am producing is a visualization of this sort. One morning, after having slept poorly, I woke with a start and witnessed, as from a seat in a theater, three acts which brought to life an epoch and characters about which I had no documentary information." This experience led to his play *The Knights of the Round Table*.

L.E. Walkup (1965) studied creative scientists. In his paper, "Creativity in Science Through Visualization" (imagery), he says, "Creative persons have stumbled onto and then developed to a high degree of perfection the ability to visualize in the area in which they are creative. And their visualizations seem to be a sort that lend themselves to easy manipulation in the thinking process."

Rollo May (1959) tells of a scientist who dreamed a formula, wakened, and in his excitement hurriedly scribbled it on a paper handkerchief only to find he could not read it the next morning. Each succeeding night he concentrated on redreaming it, and after several nights, he did. This time he got up immediately and carefully recorded the formula, for which he was awarded the Nobel Prize.

There are literally hundreds of such anecdotes, showing that imagery, dreaming, day dreaming, creativity, and creative problem solving are closely related. These altered states of consciousness have been labeled with various designations. These include "Fringe of Consciousness" (James, 1950), "Preconscious" (Kubie, 1958), "Other Conscious" and "Transliminal Mind" (Rugg, 1963), "Transliminal Experience" (Mackinnon, 1964), "Reveries" (Green, 1970).

According to leading-edge physics research, the use of altered states

...ciousness can lead to a transformation of nearly every part of your ... physical chemist Ilya Prigogine recently proposed a theory that earned him a Nobel Prize. The theory—already confirmed by experiments—is called "the theory of dissipative structures." It has solved the mystery of why the use of altered states can result in life-changing insights and new behavior patterns.

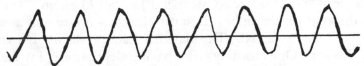

Figure 3. Beta brain-wave levels maintain a fairly constant flow of energy through the brain.

Diagram 2. Alpha and Theta brain-wave levels create large fluctuations of energy through the brain.

We have already discussed the fact that the brain is an energy system and that this energy can be measured by an EEG machine. The up-and-down pattern of brain wave levels (as indicated in figure 3) reflects a fluctuation of energy in the brain. In full, or beta consciousness, your brain wave levels would show up on the EEG graph as small, rapid, up and down liners. However, when you alter your state of consciousness through the use of imagery, meditation, breathing systematically, or deep body relaxation, your brain wave levels shift to alpha then perhaps to theta.

According to Prigogine's theory, small fluctuations of energy (such as beta rhythms) are suppressed by the brain so it stays essentially the same, (that's why changes in the form of new information, suggested to the conscious mind, have little or modest effect—the message is suppressed by all the existing programming. On the other hand, suggestions given to an individual during alpha and theta brain wave levels are more effective. This increased state of "receptiveness" is why some researchers say, "A message, a positive affirmation, a suggestion, etc. given while a person is in alpha has many times the effect, in terms of modifying behavior, than the same suggestion given while a person is in beta."

Barbara Brown (1980) discusses the condition of stress as an overload of the cerebral circuitry system in the brain. Interesting! No wonder when we are stressed it is so difficult to focus, concentrate, think logically, or creatively. "Forced thinking" is trying to solve a problem logically while the mind and body are working in disharmony.

For the past 25 years, Dr. Geogi Lozanov, has been conducting research at the Institute of Suggestology in Sofia, Bulgaria, on accelerated learning and memory. Dr. Lozanov, speculated if you could have painless surgery, and painless childbirth, why couldn't you also have the painless birth of knowledge? If techniques derived from yoga and meditation took the pain out of surgery and childbirth, why not also try then to take the pain out of learning? He refers to illness caused by poor teaching methods "Didactogeny." A major part of his approach to learning and memory has to do with a method he calls "suggestopedia."

Steps in the suggestopedia method:

Step 1 Process of De-suggestion
Lozanov referred to this as self-image therapy. We are conditioned to believe that we can only learn so much, so fast. Part of this first step is to help people to get over these limitations in thinking—that we can learn faster and release our inner potential.

Step 2 Mind and Body Relaxation
At this stage Lozanov teaches people the art of relaxing mind and body and uses a combination of breathing and imagery exercises.

Step 3 Music
After considerable psychoacoustic research Lozanov discovered that a certain type of music with a tempo of 60-70 beats a minute had a very positive effect on one's central nervous system. He discovered that certain sound patterns can affect consciousness in a very positive manner. In the slow movement of Baroque music (Bach, Vivaldi, Handel, Corelli) your body listens and tends to follow the beat. Your body relaxes and your mind becomes alert. (Later in the text I will discuss the effects of music on imagery creativity and problem solving.)

Step 4 Presentation of Material
Lozanov uses an eight-second cycle for pacing out spoken data at slow intervals. Think of the eight second cycle as two bars of four beats or two frames of four second each. Each beat is one second. 1 2 3 4 / 1 2 3 4. During the first four beats of the cycle you remain silent. During the next four beats you say the data. A twelve beat cycle has also been used with success where there were more data to be presented. You are to hold your breath while the data is being said (either by another person or a tape recorder). Different intonations are recommended for each cycle.

Years of research have demonstrated that people are able to use this technique to learn in a short period of time (a few weeks) a great deal of information. For an indepth presentation on this subject see *SUPER LEARNING* by Sheila Ostrander and Lynn Schroeder. For a Special Baroque Music List, write: Superlearning Corp., Suite 40, 17 Park Avenue, New York, N.Y. 10016.

A major finding of Lozanov's work was that a pause between data-bytes gave brain cells a chance to rest a moment so that they were better able to register the next item. Rapid fire presentation of data seemed to blur registration in the brain.

The body relaxation and the baroque music, along with a comfortable environment and a positive attitude resulted in a shift of consciousness enabling the person to go from beta to at least alpha and perhaps theta.

While a number of research studies using the Super Learning approach have been conducted in the U.S since 1968, results have not been totally positive. Perhaps a lack of proper preparation has led to failure with a potentially good method. In my imagery training, I constantly emphasize the necessity of introducing material, slowly and over a long period of time—so that frustration and failure are minimized. But despite my cautious approach, some teachers (the ones that skip this section of the reading and jump to exercises) still run back to the classroom and start with advanced imagery techniques. Please don't do that.

ACCELERATED MENTAL PROCESSING (AMP)

In this last section, I want to examine another extraordinary aspect of mind which is referred to as Accelerated Mental Processing (AMP). First coined by author, researcher, and psychologist Jean Houston, AMP is defined as the ability of increasing the rate of thought or amount of subjective experience beyond what is ordinarily possible within a unit of clock-measured time. Houston states, "under certain conditions of altered consciousness a person might experience within a few minutes, as measured by the clock, such a wealth of ideas or images that it will seem that hours, days or even longer must have passed for him to have experienced so much." Houston says, "it has long been known that AMP occurs spontaneously under conditions of dreaming sleep (the 'hours long' dream that takes only a few seconds or minutes of clock time) or how about the stories told by people who have experienced near death situations and claim that before their eyes all the significant lifetime events were flashed in an instant. It is important to note that in all of the above mentioned experiences of AMP, imagery plays a predominant role. Imagistic thinking does not seem to be bound by the time-inhibited mechanisms which retard the flow of verbal thought.

One of the approaches in teaching people the potential of AMP is to tell them that their normal rate of thought or subjective experience is very much slower than need be. Secondly you tell them that they have a specific amount of clock time (30 seconds, a minute) for the image experience. What you are doing, is priming, conditioning your people for maximum performance. I have noticed from my own work with AMP that most people are able to evoke and control their images easier and faster. They also concentrate better. When later asked about the procedure of specifying clock time, several persons told me that it helped them stay with the image, i.e., it helped them stay in synch! Houston found, that her subjects were able to experience a fairly elaborate adventure story within a brief unit of clock-measured time. She reported that of 486 subjects who participated in AMP experiments, only 27 have had subjective experiences which they thought lasted a minute or less. Most felt that their experience (which was one minute) lasted from about five to 40 minutes. The implication from these results are fascinating. We have really just started to study AMP in relationship to learning and problem solving. In Chapters 3 and 4 the reader will find a more in depth presentation of imagery and its uses.

CHAPTER 3

IMAGE CREATION AND PROBLEM SOLVING

"Those who dream by night in the dusty recesses of their minds wake in the day to find that it was vanity; but the dreamers of the day are dangerous men, for they may act their dreams with open eyes, to make it possible."

T. E. Lawrence

Having reviewed some of the basic issues related to creativity, and having explored areas of human potential, let us now begin focusing our attention on the image and how this phenomenon is used in creative problem solving. The basic aim of this chapter is to: (a) discuss the nature of imagery (b) discuss why imagery is such a valuable tool in creative problem solving (c) provide a framework for using imagery in creative problem solving in the classroom (d) offer suggestions for increasing students imaging skills and (e) show how imagery and problem solving foster creative expression.

WHAT IS IMAGERY?

The image has been identified in psychological literature as a vision, as a source for new thought and feeling, as a material picture in the mind which can be scanned by the person as s/he would scan a real current event in his/her environment, and as a potent, highly significant stimulus which arises from within the mind and throws it into a series of self-revealing effects (Richardson, 1968, Ahsen, 1977). It is a method which uses spontaneous and multi-potential images (pictures) instead of words for exposure to new life-related emotions and ideas. Imagery is an ideation process which is fundamentally different from forced thinking. A relaxed mind generates its own ideas, and the distinguishing feature of such ideas is that they are invariably energizing and potent. Through image creating one can make an experience (problem situation) run slowly, generate more detail and get a much better grip of the event. An experience running at less than half its usual speed is obviously more analyzable and for the same reason, more manageable i.e., we become a projectionist capable of speeding up, stilling or slowing down various images. This imaging process surfaces information which verbal/logical thinking may be unable to produce on demand. The image is noted for its perceptual qualities, persistence and clarity of detail. It provides optimum concreteness to the visualizer because it can be evoked and experienced over and over again in a vivid manner and can be scanned. The image consists of three major components: The (I) image which is the picture; the (S) somatic response, which is the emotional or feeling message received from the images; and the (M) meaning, which is the conceptual idea, perception or new thought generated (Ashen, 1977). Imagery is a highly "creative act" most effective for gaining new ideas, strengthening the self-concept and relaxing the mind and body. The image process has no boundaries, it can be used to increase one's basic knowledge, level of understanding and sensitivity to all human events. To that extent, we are talking about, perhaps man's greatest human capacity. According to Norman Vincent Peale in his latest book, *Positive Imaging*, "Imaging is positive thinking one step further."

Albert Einstein wrote (1925) that words did not play a role in his thought—the psychical entities which seem to serve as elements in thought are certain signs and more or less clear images which can be "voluntarily" reproduced and combined.

IMAGES IN OUR DREAMS AND DAYDREAMS

The average person has approximately four to five dreams per night. Although many individuals do not recall dreaming, nevertheless it has been clearly established that each of us spends twenty percent of the night projecting various pictures (dreams) in our mind's eye—and that this process is automatic. Dream researchers have discovered techniques to influence this natural process. "Plan and control your dreams for a more creative and anxiety-free life" says Dr. Patricia Garfield in her book *Creative Dreaming*, 1974. She teachers people strategies for dream planning, dream recording (through the use of dream diaries) and dream analysis. In Chapter 4, one of our creative problem solving strategies has to do with dreams.

In addition to seeing pictures in our mind's eye each night, many of us experience images in the form of daydreams. The amount of daydreaming one does relates to a number of factors, such as, personality, environmental stimuli, time, etc. Like dreams, daydreams seem to just pop into our consciousness, in an unexpected manner. In both dreams and daydreams the imaging process is "involuntary" that is, the pictures begin without our conscious request—"they just happen." This is a normal occurrence that each of us experiences to varying degrees. Therefore, it is safe to say that the innate ability to see pictures in the mind's eye (in the form of dreams and daydreams) is something that the human being possesses.

However, quite different from this natural process is the "voluntary" activation and control of the image. Here lie the major differences. In dreaming, which is considered to be our most vivid type of image, we have little to do with the imaging process. When we intentionally decide to evoke an image, a whole different process and skill comes into play. It is this voluntary imaging skill, i.e., image creation, that is the focus of the creative problem solving training program.

OTHER TYPES OF IMAGES

One of the most popular types of imagery is the **MEMORY IMAGE**. A person may be able to call actively upon a previous experience in attempting to remember certain facts or details. Memory images are usually evoked by a sensory stimulus, a verbal utterance, a picture, a certain taste, or a smell. Someone will say something, and all of a sudden we are pulling out old memories. The verbal utterance triggers the mind to activate in the form of mental pictures (memory images) of an event, situation or experience that could have happened a long time ago. When we focus our attention and increase our motivation, the flow of memory images will continue as long as our concentration and interest last. Try this activity. After you read these next few lines, close your eyes and just allow some memory images to float into your awareness. Alright. Remember one of your favorite elementary school teachers. Imagine that person standing in front of his/her classroom. Notice the way the person is dressed. Now allow your eyes to move slowly down the person observing every detail. Now I want you to see, very clearly, that person's shoes.

How did you do? Some of you haven't thought of that person in 20, 30 perhaps 40 years, yet in seconds you were able to access very clear and vivid images. Another activity you can try is to have an adult friend close his or her eyes, relax, and listen as you suggest the following:

See yourself standing in the middle of a childhood room ... notice the wall in front of you ... the wall to one side ... now the other wall ... see a window and the window covering ... now find something in this room that brought you great pleasure ... see it clearly, all its details ... now just fade out of the image.

I always enjoy listening to the types of objects or experiences people focused on during this activity. Most individuals will be able to see quite clearly something that brought them great pleasure—even if they haven't thought of it in fifty years. Both of these activities clearly demonstrate the nature of memory imaging as well as our inner capacity for storing information.

Dr. Lozanov's research convinced him that, in a sense, we already have supermemory. The problem is we can't recall what we store away. "The human mind remembers a colossal quantity of information," he says, "the number of buttons on a suit, steps on a staircase, panes in a window, footsteps to the bus stop." These "unknown perceptions" show us the subconscious has startling powers.

Dr. Wilder Penfield of the Montreal Neurological Institute backs up this idea. He says, "we have a kind of natural built-in 'tape recorder' in our heads." Penfield theorizes, "EVERY experience—sight, sound, smell, and taste—registers as a particular pattern in the brain and that this pattern stays on long after the experience is consciously forgotten."

Another type of image is IMAGINATION IMAGERY. It is different from the memory image in that it has no fixed reference point. It does not necessarily relate to a specific event or situation. Imagination images are spontaneous, free, unstructured, creative experiences integrating the past and present in newly organized patterns. It is creative imagery that often provides the artist or poet with the central idea for a picture or poem (Richardson, 1969). Vincent Van Gogh once wrote to his brother Theo, "I have a lover's clear sight or a lover's blindness .... I shall do another picture this very night, and I shall bring it off. I have a terrible lucidity at moments when nature is so beautiful; I am not conscious of myself any more, and the pictures come to me as in a dream." There are many such anecdotes demonstrating the nature of imagination, through which the individual receives a steady flow of creative images.

It is imagination imagery that is the cornerstone of our creative problem solving approach. It is, perhaps the most difficult since it requires a "letting go" of rational and linear thought processes. I am convinced, however, that imagination imagery is the most important feature of image

g. Once people begin to trust and successfully explore the pos-
siblities of imagination imagery, they will experience increasing pleasures
and considerable insight into its vast potential. All of the creative problem
solving imagery techniques in Chapter 4 are of the imagination image
type. A more in depth discussion can be found later in that section of
the text.

The final type of image is the **EIDETIC IMAGE**. Most researchers
believe that the eidetic image is an image of unusual vividness. A. Ahsen
(l977) believes that many people are capable of experiencing this especially
vivid and detailed image than was previously thought. Ahsen claims in
his fascinating book, *Psyche* (1977), "Memory image is always open to
arbitrary change but that eidetic image is closed to arbitrary change or
revision but subject to further progression in a definite direction, i.e., it
is corrective in nature." It is the eidetic image process that many
psychologists are presently using in therapy.

MAJOR COMPONENTS OF THE IMAGE PROCESS

As I stated earlier, the image process consists of three major components.
They are (I) image (pictures), (S) somatic response and (M) meaning.
It is very important that you understand that imagery is a process that
once learned and mastered can be applied to any form of learning or
problem solving. Let us now take a more in depth look at Ahsen's ISM
paradigm.

(I) Image (picture)
The first part of the process deals with the picture (visual) a person
evokes while imaging. The picture may come in any shade, color, form
or shape and may be seen as if you were looking through a misty screen,
or it may be vivid and life-like in all its features and distinctions. As I
will discuss later, the ability to see images clearly depends on many
variables, including motivation, interest, degree of trust, guidance, content, setting, body position, etc. These variables will be discussed in a
later question and answer section. The image (picture) will stay in the
mind's eye for as long as the person maintains a high degree of concentration. Once the imager loses interest, the picture will fade and perhaps
be lost. The key to evoking vivid pictures is to let them evolve slowly
and naturally, never forcing or fighting the image. Evoking the image
requires an effortless approach—to force is to lose.

(S) Somatic (feeling)
As the image (Picture) is maintained the imager begins to receive emo-

tional messages in the form of subjective feelings. These somatic responses may take the form of such feelings as joy, fear, enthusiasm, happiness, excitement etc. These responses often act as a reinforcing mechanism for continued image projection or may serve as a signal to discontinue image content. The emotional reaction is important because it serves as a motivator, helping to maintain a high level of concentration. It also helps in the "mental imprinting" process—what is seen, is stored, and remembered—thus making it easier for later recall. As the picture is maintained through conscious control and supported through a steady flow of somatic responses, the imager begins to register in the form of thoughts and perceptions different meanings about the content being seen in their minds' eye.

Meaning (cognition)

The final part of the process is meaning. As the imager focuses on the mind's visual material and continues receiving emotional responses, messages are received in the form of thought patterns, meanings about the content being projected. Image theorists, believe that meanings generated through vivid images are much more accurate and revealing than meanings obtained through verbal processes. The latter process has to deal with conscious bias and prejudices and all sorts of filtering devices—meanings obtained via images are pure and uncontaminated. This realization of the superiority of meanings from images is often expressed by individuals engaged in imagery activities.

It is important that the reader understand the ISM process, as it is especially relevant to the work we will be doing in creative problem solving. When evoking images relating to problem situations you will be continually activating the ISM process. Essentially, you will be going into image, out of image, into image, and out of image. While out of image you will be asked to describe the ISM in action, in terms of the nature of your visualizations, the level and degree of emotional reactions and the different meanings received.

The success to creative problem solving will depend on how easily you work within the structure of the ISM.

RATIONALE FOR IMAGERY IN THE CLASSROOM

- It is a natural tendency for individuals to think in visual images.
- In every class there are at least 20 to 30% of the students who are by birth more inclined to visual thinking than verbal thinking.
- Researchers have found that the image is our most potent tool for

gaining access to our innate creative mind.

- Psychologists have identified a close and significant relationship between imagination and health.
- Scientists and medical doctors both agree that guided imagery has a strong relaxation effect beneficial to one's health.
- Imagery is perhaps the easiest manner for having children experience the creative process.
- Imagery has been the major focus of research study in the field of creativity for the last 10 years.
- Imagery (visual thinking) is needed to balance our thinking process.
- Imagery is a major psycho-technology being used in:
  medicine
  business
  healing
  sports
  education
  arts.
- Initial studies demonstrate that imagery has not only a positive effect on enhancing learning skills but has an equally positive effect on social and emotional behaviors of students.

THE ROLE OF GUIDED AND NON-GUIDED IMAGERY

In my early work with imagery, I primarily focused on different types of guided images that could be used in the classroom. In fact, most of the image exercises in *200 Ways of Using Imagery in The Classroom* are guided image activities. Our thinking (Bagley & Hess, 1982) was that imagery was a new process, and we wanted to be sure that teachers and students were able to adjust to the image way of thinking and learning. It was our belief that the guided image was the best overall approach to achieve that goal. The guided image is especially effective when dealing with important academic subject matter.

During the last few years having gone through thousands of imagery experiences, I'm finding that the non-guided imagery has a whole world of creative potential. Within its realm, image creation was designed to combine both guided and non-guided imagery. The CPS exercises are guided only to a certain extent. Each exercise has several opportunities for the imager to conjure up and project his/her own images. Image creation represents a model, an approach to unlocking one's inner creative abilities. Some students prefer guided images, others prefer non-guided with perhaps some background music. However, when introducing imagery, most beginning exercises should be of the guided variety. After a few short exercises, work in some short non-guided exercises. For example, select an image content such as ocean waves. Tell the students you will give them 30 seconds to image ocean waves; the students will have complete freedom to focus in on any aspect of that theme.

To teach students only through guided imagery is a big mistake that we cannot afford to make. The imagery we use in life is primarily non-guided. Therefore it is crucial that our students understand the importance of both guided and non-guided imagery. We must encourage them constantly to explore their own imagery for different purposes, in different situations.

WHY IS THE IMAGE A "NATURAL TOOL" FOR CREATIVE PROBLEM SOLVING ?

First, imagery is closer to direct experience than verbal thought. Words are usually labels to describe an experience whereas an image involves reliving the experience. The image enables people to develop the ability to look at an object from different points of view, as well as from different physical vantage points. This process of rapidly shifting viewpoints helps people break free of their habitual ways of seeing things. Another consideration which was presented in our discussion of ISM, is that the image involves the whole physiological system and allows various senses and physiological sectors to participate in a spontaneous manner. According to Dr. Edward DeBono (1975), "Any attempt to increase creative behavior depends for its success on interfering with the natural behavior of the information processing system." Creating images is perhaps the easiest way of interfering with this normal processing system. The image which is a "creative act" in itself, has a natural inclination to draw upon its infinite imagination, in distorting, inverting, transposing an object, thing or situation. Break through depends on strange new contexts.

It is precisely this issue of being free to interfere with our conditioned information processing system that needs to be reinforced in our schools. Vertical thinking and indeed the whole system of education is based on the principle that one must not be wrong—the very essence of logic is that one cannot proceed by means of an unjustified step. Yet the fear of doing wrong is the biggest barrier there is to new ideas. The imagery process is the best means for breaking this over dependency on vertical thinking.

One of the most fascinating characteristics of imagery is the "principle of repetition," (Ahsen, 1977). Every time an image is repeated, the imager will receive a different perspective. It's an automatic process that continues as long as interest is maintained. Try it. Put down the book and try 3 repeated images of the theme "falling rain drops on leaves."

Project each image for approximately 15 seconds (don't worry about being exact). Pause between each image projection. Did you feel the automatic process working? If you did 100 consecutive image projections, you would continue to yield new or different perspectives.

HOW IS IMAGE CREATION DIFFERENT FROM TRADITIONAL CREATIVE PROBLEM-SOLVING APPROACHES?

Image creation is a process, which combines, integrates, and synthesizes the various principles and concepts found in traditional CPS theories and models. It's a process that uses the natural power of imagination in an unforced manner. Unlike many traditional CPS approaches, image creation does not rely only on verbal signals, materials, games, other people, written stimuli, etc. All the action takes place in the mind of the imager. It is the imager, who by evoking, manipulating, transforming and creating different images, unlocks the doors to imagination and creative problem solving. Dr. Jean Houston (1980) found that it is possible to increase greatly the rate of thought or amount of subjective experience beyond what is ordinarily possible within a unit of clock-measured time. It is evident that thinking need not be limited by the slow pace of our physiological being or by the linear inhibitions of our verbal thought. She goes on to say, "Creative people who think in images, find solutions and express ideas that are not possible when the thinking is purely verbal." Image production allows one to tape the massive, infinite mental library of the subconscious mind. According to Dr. Sidney Parnes, observation and manipulation go hand-in-hand, i.e., the more observations we make about an object or situation, the more manipulations are possible and the more new configurations (ideas-solutions) we are able to formulate. As Dr. A. Ahsen has said "The image is the lightening rod of human energy." The image process is an accelerated version of the Theory of Synectics. In synectics, the idea is to take a familiar problem and make it strange, i.e., take a new and different perspective in looking at the problem. Through different analogies (personal-direct and fantasy) a synectics participant will engage in such activities as role playing, brainstorming, listing, divergent thinking, etc. The aim is to free the mind from traditional, linear ways of seeing things.

Imagery is similar in that the process allows the imager to look at a familiar problem in a strange new way. However, the range of diversified thought and the potential for creativity is far superior. The role playing, brainstorming, mental manipulations, assoications, emotions, are all performed in "lightning speed" taking advantage of accelerated mental processing.

It is not that traditional Creative Problem Solving approaches are inferior, but Creative Problem Solving Imagery is a superior methodology with unlimited potential.

SPECIFIC ADVANTAGES OF USING IMAGERY IN CREATIVE PROBLEM SOLVING

1. It eases irrelevant tension which enables greater concentration on the Target Problem.
2. The image is the fastest, easiest means for tapping our creative potential.
3. Imagery does not depend on purely verbal thinking which can be limited by the slow pace of our physiological being.
4. Imagery does not depend on external resources such as charts, lists, other people, games, etc.
5. There's no limit to the number of manipulations that can be performed on any image content.
6. The image process has a strong emotional component and, according to Dr. Gordon (1976), "In the creative process, the emotional component is more important than the rational."
7. Imagery can be done alone, in private. It doesn't require large groups of people.
8. Imagery increases the rate of thought or amount of subjective experience beyond what is ordinarily possible within a unit of clock-measured time. (AMP).
9. Imagery has a "can't fail" aspect to it since there really isn't any one exact way to image something—everybody succeeds—nobody fails!
10. Imagery is fun! It has an energizing, refueling-of-self component that makes one "feel good."

Constructing the "CPS-Workshop"

What is a Mental Workshop?

The workshop is a specific setting (room, building, laboratory, etc.) which is created in the student's mind for the purpose of assisting in creative problem solving activities. The workshop provides the imager with a familiar environment that is conducive to relaxation, excellent for maintaining concentration and manipulation. Using the Workshop Image (guided instructions below), the teacher guides the students in the designing, building and decorating of his/her own workshop. The students are encouraged to make their workshop pleasant, comfortable and consistent with their taste. The students are free to change or modify any dimension of their workshop at any time.

How is the workshop used?

After the students have successfully built their workshops the teacher may then conduct any of the creative problem solving exercises presented in Chapter 4, or any additional exercises developed by the teacher or students. All of the CPS exercises originate in the students workshop. Once in the workshop, it is quite easy to shift mental gears and through concentration begin imaging anything you desire, e.g., traveling around the world, going into outer space, walking on a beach, talking to a famous person, etc. After the creative exercise the student is instructed to return to his/her workshop—and then finally back to his original setting, which is usually the classroom. The CPS exercises all have specific instructions for entering or leaving the workshop. After practice most people find it quite easy to go in-and-out out the workshop.

How long should a workshop exercise be?

Most of the CPS exercises are between ten and fifteen minutes which is an appropriate length of time for a specific exercise. However, some of the exercises require thirty minutes. The longer exercises shouldn't be used until the students are comfortable with the process. Sustained concentration for a thirty-minute period requires a good deal of skill. As you use and explore the workshop techniques, you will find that you become the best one to judge just how long the experience should be. Other variables to consider are: setting, number of distractions, time of day, class activity just completed, use of stimuli, e.g., music, etc.

How often should the workshop exercise be used?

After observing elementary teachers use the workshop for a period of one year, my colleagues and I agreed that twice a week was best. By doing the activity twice per week, it keeps the students imaging skills sharpened and in tune. Remember, image creation is a skill and if nurtured properly, it can become a rich natural resource..

Should students use their Idea Workbooks following a CPS exercise?

Definitely yes! To express creative work is just as important as the act of generating it through images and thoughts. At least five minutes should be given to students at the end of the workshop for entering data into their Idea Workbooks. Some exercises require students to spend more time working with their Idea Workbooks. Taking abstract ideas, conceptualizations and putting them into a concrete format is a powerful teaching tool. The Idea books are not generally shared as the content can be very personal. However, if the student would like to discuss an issue or problem with the teacher it should be most acceptable. Students should be encouraged to use their Idea books freely—this means weekends, vacations, etc. Occasionally I will get a letter from a former graduate student who in turn received a letter from an elementary student describing how s/he used the Idea Workbook during the summer.

Workshop Rules:

1) Students *do not* have to do a workshop exercise if they feel uncomfortable about a particular Target Problem at that point in time. It's O.K. to just sit quietly until the exercise is over.
2) Silence is a *must* during workshop exercises—distractions, noise, talking, etc., will break the group's concentration.
3) Students should be permitted to sit at their desks, lie on the floor, go off to a special area of the room, or any other personal preference area.
4) Idea Workbooks should be used after CPS-Imagery exercises (sometimes it can be put off until schedule permits).
5) *Always* provide at least a few minutes for group discussion following CPS-Imagery exercises (often, students have questions or points of

clarifications).

6) Students *do not* have to close their eyes during workshop exercises as some of our highly imaginative individuals can image and concentrate better with eyes open—however most people will find eyes open to be distracting.

7) Can students guide other students through CPS guided imagery exercises? Yes, providing the teacher has reviewed the students guided imagery script (written statements), and only after the class had had sufficient exposure to the process.

8) Put an *In Workshop* or *Imaging* sign on the outside of the classroom door to alert visitors.

9) *Never* force a student to share their CPS imagery experience.

Why is it necessary to count the group back from an imagery exercise?

Imagery is a relaxing process that literally slows down our brain energy. When that brain energy slows down and our minds become fixed on the object of our visualization, we tend to fade-out of our normal state of awareness. This causes the body to slow its metabolism (heart rate slows, oxygen consumption decreases, etc.) and the brain to ease energy production within the circuitry system. Therefore, when the image is complete we need a few seconds to increase body metabolism to its normal state and to return the brain to its normal energy production. Some imagers reduce brain energy to lower levels—thus requiring a few seconds to return to normal firing or our alet state of awareness. If a youngster is tired, s/he might even fall asleep during an imagery exercise.

The count back is a way to extend courtesy to any students who need that extra second or two to return from the image experience. The more you work with imagery, the more you will be able to judge the manner in which you bring students back to regular focus and the number of seconds it will take. Practice, practice, practice!

CPS WORKSHOP
TERMS AND CONCEPTS

CREATIVE WORKSHOP—A mental laboratory, a special room or environment which is relaxing, comfortable and appropriate for experiencing imagery. The workshop is created through a guided image found in this later chapter.

IMAGE PROJECTION—The process of projecting (evoking) an image onto one's viewing screen which is the mind's eye. The projection concept is used to reinforce the idea that the imager is like a projectionist capable of speeding up, slowing down, stilling, reversing, etc., an image.

IMAGER—usually refers to a student participating in one of the CPS exercises. It means that s/he is engaged in the image process, actively projecting images (pictures) on his/her viewing screen.

IMAGE SET—A verbal cue signifying that the guided image exercise is to begin. It alerts the imager that the next set of guided instructions will pertain to the image content.

PROJECTION SCREEN—A large screen created during the work-shop guided image. It will be used for image projecting. The same screen should be used so that the imager becomes familiar and comfortable with it.

VIEWING CHAIR—A large comfortable chair created during the workshop guided image. It is the recommended viewing chair where the imager conducts the CPS exercises.

PAUSE = **P**—In each of the CPS Imagery Exercises you will find the symbol (P) indicating that there is a recommended pause at that moment. The teacher remains silent for the length of time indicated after the P, e.g., P = 60 sec.

FADE-IN—The process of having an image slowly come into focus.

FADE-OUT—The process of having an image slowly dissolve or disappear from one's viewing screen.

TARGET PROBLEM (TP)—The TP is the specific problem area or concern a person selects for a particular CPS imagery exercise. The TP may change depending on the CPS exercise or the person may wish to use the same TP for all CPS exercises.

Workshop Image...Guided Instructions

Teacher Instructions:

Building the workshop is an important first step in the Image Creation approach to problem solving. Therefore the guided image which follows must be done in one sitting, with little or no interruptions and must be presented in the highest professional manner. *Guiding students through images is an art requiring great skill, patience and discipline.* Teachers should practice this exercise several times prior to administering the image to the class. During this practice period the teacher should be exposing the students to various types of instructional images. Once comfortable with the process, the teacher is then ready to do the following guided Workshop Image. Please be sure to describe the process to the students prior to the image exercise.

Guided Workshop Image Instructions:
— Find a comfortable position, relax and begin focusing on your breathing
   P = 15 sec.
— You're letting go of all thoughts
— Just focus on your relaxed breathing
— There is lots of time
— You are starting to feel calm and comfortable
— Alright...with your imagination I want you to build a special workshop room
— You are the architect, builder and designer
— You can construct this workshop using any materials, textures, colors, etc., of your choice
— Let us begin
— Very slowly I want you to see the foundation being constructed
— Notice the size, shape, materials you are using
— Begin to see the foundation floor
— Remember—this is your workshop, make it exactly how you would like it to be
— Next . . . observe the outer walls being constructed
— Now the roof
— Now the interior walls—just see clearly, the type of walls you are building P = 15 sec.
— Observe the ceiling and all its detail
— You are beginning to experience a special feeling about your workshop

— Now take a moment and begin decorating your workshop—just feel free to put whatever you'd like into your workshop—make it satisfying to you P = 30 sec.
— Alright...stop for a moment as I want you to add three things to your workshop
— First, I want you to see a large, soft, comfortable chair
— Notice its size, shape, color, texture
— This is your special Viewing Chair
— Next I want you to see a large screen directly across from your chair
— Notice its detail
— See it clearly
— This screen will serve as your special Viewing Screen where you will create your future images
— Finally, I want you to see another chair that will be your assistant's chair
— Alright...now see if there are any other items you would like to put in your workshop
— Now take a moment and just look around your workshop; see clearly everything you have created—colors—textures—
— Feel how relaxing and special your Workshop is
— You have created your own Workshop
— You may come back to your Workshop at any time and make any changes you would like
— So take all these images with you now as you prepare to leave your Workshop P = 15 sec.
— I want you to now begin to focus on images of your original classroom setting
— When I count to ten you will be back in your classroom, alert and ready to go!
— One...five, six...ten...you're back and very alert!

NOTE: Ask students to describe their workshop experience in the Idea Workbooks. Allow at least 15 minutes. Follow this with a discussion period, primarily on the process. DON'T *MAKE* STUDENTS TELL ABOUT THEIR WORKSHOPS. If students would *like* to share their workshop experience—then that is fine!

The Workshop is like an artistic drawing—not all people immediately like to share—respect this!

Since the students have established their Workshops, it is not necessary to recreate them—just follow the guided instructions presented with each CPS exercise. If some students were not able to create a Workshop, then perhaps you could do the exercise again for a smaller group or even for an individual.

Encourage the students to make changes in their Workshops. Anything goes (swimming pools, pool tables, T.V., soda fountain, etc.). Remember this is imagination—so let it happen!

What is the CPS-Idea Workbook?

The Idea Workbook is a very important feature of the creative problem solving process. It represents a concrete, tangible, component where students can write and draw about their thoughts, ideas, and feelings in a non-judgmental way. The book is personal and should be respected and treated in that manner. There are suggestions at the end of each CPS-Imagery exercise in Chapter 4 for ways students can use their workbooks for follow-up assignments to image experiences. Students should be encouraged to use the workbook whenever the schedule or time permits.

CPS-Idea Workbook Rules

1. Students *do not* have to share the content of the books unless they so desire.
2. Never judge or evaluate the content of an Idea Workbook.
3. Encourage *free* use of Idea Workbooks, e.g., during free time, on weekends, etc.
4. Following CPS-Imagery Exercises allow students time for using Workbooks, even if it's only 5 minutes.
5. Discuss the Idea Workbook with parents, perhaps during open house. Encourage them to follow the *privacy rule.*
6. Make the CPS-Idea Workbook an important part of your weekly schedule.

RELAXATION

Body relaxation is the first step in learning how to improve the ability to image. Conscious relaxation removes extraneous stimuli, thereby allowing a person to concentrate more intensely on his inner state. Body relaxation has been found by several researchers to facilitate the flow of internal images. According to researcher Dr. Elmer Green, "Truly creative thinking takes place when the mind is in a state of inner calm"—in other words, the great and creative discoveries is science, in the arts, in the corporate office generally come at times when the mind is at peace with itself. Imagery can create this inner state of peace.

The first tenet of learning a new skill in any field is relaxation. The skilled always "make it seem easy," The second tenet is complete attention. Relaxation and attention are mutually supportive and lead to good image production. By relaxing irrelevant tension, the individual releases full energy and attention to the task at hand. A relaxed mind is a requisite to concentration. Relaxation is key to imaging and thinking generally, because we image and think with our whole being, our body as well as our brain. Overly tense muscles divert attention, restrict circulation of blood, waste energy, stress the nervous system: uptight body, uptight thoughts. The ability to relax attentively is especially important to imaging. Excessive eye tension interferes with the natural flow of images.

The following exercises can be used to relax the students prior to going into their Creative Workshops and/or doing CPS-imagery exercises.

RELAXATION EXERCISE: 1
Diaphragmatic Breathing

Guided Instructions:
— Sit comfortably and relax P[ause] = 5 sec.
— Keep your spine straight and your feet flat on the floor P = 5 sec.
— Let your hands lie comfortably on your lap P = 5 sec.
— Now take a deep breath and slowly exhale P = 10 sec.
— You're letting go of all thoughts. P = 5 sec.
— Again take another deep breath and slowly exhale P = 10 sec.
— There is lots of time P = 10 sec.
— Concentrate on the air flowing in and out of your nostrils P = 15 sec.
— Coolness on inhalation — warmth on exhalation P = 3 sec.
— Just take a minute and sense this gentle air flow P = 30 sec.
— Now let us focus on your diaphragm muscle which is just below your lungs. Note: (it would be good to show class a picture of the anatomy of the lungs and diaphragm muscle.)
— Notice as you inhale your diaphragm pushing downward forcing your stomach cavity to thrust outward and as you exhale feel your diaphragm moving upward like a parachute.
— Take a moment and observe this relaxing action. Stomach out on exhalation—stomach in on inhalation P = 60 sec.
— You now feel calm and comfortable P = 5 sec.
— Your breathing is slow and easy P = 10 sec.
— Just continue to focus on your relaxing breathing P = 2 mins.
— Alright . . . you have completed your relaxing breathing exercise P = 5 sec.
— Slowly begin to focus on images of our original setting P = 5 sec.
— When I count to ten you will be alert and fully energized.
— One —— three —— . . . wide awake.

RELAXATION EXERCISE: 2
Systematic Body Relaxation

Guided Instructions:
— Find a comfortable position, sit comfortably, and relax.
— Keep your spine straight and feet flat on the floor.
— Take a deep breath and slowly relax P = 15 sec.
— Allow your thoughts to leave P = 10 sec.
— You have lots of time P = 15 sec.
— I want you to focus all your attention on your feet and say, "My feet are becoming relaxed." P = 15 sec.
— Now in the same manner relax your ankles P = 7 sec.
— Just feel the relaxation moving up into your lower legs P = 10 sec.
— Now have the relaxing power move up into your upper legs letting all the muscles of your legs completely relax P = 15 sec.
— You feel the relaxation in your hip and pelvic area P = 15 sec.
— Now have the relaxation move up into your stomach relaxing all the muscles P = 15 sec.
— And now just feel the relaxation moving into your chest as all the muscles of your chest completely relax.
— Direct this relaxation down one of your arms just feel the relaxation moving slowly, slowly, down, down your arm P = 5 sec.
— Feel the tensions leave through your finger tips P = 7 sec.
— Now your other arm, just feel the relaxation moving slowly down your arm—as the tensions leave through your finger tips P = 7 sec.
— Now focus your attention to your neck and shoulder area and allow this relaxing power to penetrate all the muscles as you just feel the tightness and tensions leave. And the relaxation slowly moves up the back of your head—up and over your head—and now coming over your forehead.
— Just feel all the muscles of your forehead and around your eyes just completely relaxing.
— Feel all the tiny muscles of the face — relaxing.
— Allow your jaw to gently drop as the relaxation covers your entire face.
— You are now calm and comfortable.
— Go back over your entire body and find any tensions spots that still might be there — and let them go.
— You are now deeply relaxed, feeling quiet and peace.
— Take a few moments and allow your mind to capture images of a beautiful, relaxing vacation spot P = 3 mins.

— Alright slowly leave this beautiful area and begin to focus on images of your original setting $P = 5$ sec.
— When I count to ten you will be safely back in your classrooms feeling refreshed and energized.
— One — three —— ... ten — wide awake.

These relaxation exercises can be lengthened or shortened depending upon your objective. They can also be combined. Pauses can be as long or as short as you like. As always, suggestions can be changed, modified, or eliminated completely. You have complete freedom to create your own style and I encourage you to do so. Just remember: keep all suggestions safe and positive. There is absolutely no need for negative feelings or violence in our imagery.

PRINCIPLES FOR ALLOWING IMAGERY TO HAPPEN

Producing images at will is a sensitive process. You can't force an image to appear. You must let the image appear. I have observed too many individuals who with good intentions, anxiously demanded the image to appear "now," Their attitude was too forceful—it just doesn't work that way. We have an "impatience" in our culture that carries over to something as subtle as evoking an image.

After much thought and discussion I finally came up with LET, WAIT & FLOW. The first concept **LET**, suggests that the imager allow the process to happen. The let attitude signifies that you are aware of the fact that the images are available and ready to come forth in an effortless manner. You have the capability and all the creative power you need for the image to project itself onto the screen of your mind's eye. You don't need to get psyched, flex your muscles, hold your breath, push, etc. In a very low-keyed, receptive manner, you just let the image float, like a cloud, into your conscious awareness.

The next concept is **WAIT**. The image will automatically appear once the brain selects the topic or content to be imaged, providing you are in a state of readiness. If the mind is preoccupied with something else, distracted by some environmental stimuli, and not in a state of relaxed focus, the image may not appear immediately. That's when the imager must be patient, take a deep breath, let go of the command and just wait passively. In a a brief second, the image will just flow onto your screen.

Point: While waiting for an image to develop, always go to your breathing—just focus in on your relaxed breathing, soon the image will follow.

The final concept is **FLOW**. Images are very gentle and have a floating nature to them. An image flows onto your screen. As you concentrate on one image, another image will just float into your awareness, and may just as quickly and freely float out of your awareness. That's why I tell people, if a negative image appears just let it flow off your screen—

43

don't pay any attention to it.

If you develop the let-wait-flow attitude, your imagery will improve considerably. However, you may have to spend some time practicing and reinforcing the concepts.

"A metaphoric way of putting it is to say that the conscious mind plants the idea in the subconscious and then allows nature to take its course without interference—that is passive volition. The operational idea suggested by the *conscious plant* is analagous to farming. The farmer a) desires and visualizes the crop b) plants the seed in the earth c) allows nature to take its course and d) reaps—In a corresponding way we a) desire a certain kind of behavior b) plant the idea in the subconscious, the earth of our psychological being c) let nature take its course (we must allow our psycho-physiological machinery to function naturally without anxiety or analytically picking at what we are trying to do, just as the farmer does not dig up his seeds to see if they are sprouting) and d) reap mind-body stability, in the form of an image, idea, etc."

Dr. Elmer Green

Image creation is a natural process that we have learned to interfere with through anxiety, anxiousness and impatience. In Dr. Green's farming metaphor, the farmer planted the seed and then relaxed and waited for the plant to grow. In imagery, your conscious mind gives the idea or image content to your *Mental Library* or *Bio-Computer* (subconscious information storage area) system—then literally just waits for the image to be produced, reaped and realized. What you are doing is letting your mental library receive instructions in a relaxed, unbiased, uncontaminated manner. Your Mental Library, Bio-Computer system does not appreciate anxious-type commands that are made in a demanding, *NOW* oriented way. Your inner machinery is very sensitive to stress, tension and an *urgency-type* behavior. If the farmer sat by his seed and demanded it to grow (over watering it) the plant might respond by dying or doing the opposite of what the farmer desired. So it is with imagery, if you demand and force an image to reap, chances are it will not surface—leading to greater anxiety. The key is to make your request (plant the seed) and just wait for the image to flow into your awareness. We *Let* the natural process happen—we *Wait* for it to happen and we observe it *Flow* onto our mind's eye.

More than 20% of every class will have a biological tendency to interfere with the Let-Wait-Flow process. These individuals really need to understand the importance of allowing imagery to happen. This is why imagery discussions are so valuable, people learn from each other—we learn how someone imaged a particular object or how someone was not able to conjure-up the image. The successes and failures of image creating is how we learn about this amazing process—not from books—although books can help.

SUGGESTIONS FOR ENHANCING THE SKILL OF IMAGING

a) Create a non-judgmental, safe, open, trusting environment.
b) Show respect and demonstrate the importance of imagination in life.
c) Introduce imagery in a small, successful steps.
d) Allow time for students to discuss various imagery experiences.
e) Treat unusual and weird ideas with respect.
f) Allow students to use the image in as many different school related areas as you can.
g) Be patient with those who need more time in acquiring imaging skills.
h) Share with students how artists, poets, writers, business persons, engineers, advertisers, athletes, doctors use imagery in their work.
i) Encourage students to image on their own.
j) Let students know that guided imagery is only one small part of image potential.
k) Discuss the image process with your students. Let them know about the different models that explain imagery (see Bagley & Hess, 1982).
l) Emphasize the let-wait-flow dimension of imagery.
m) Encourage the students to create and write guided images and then to share them with the class.
n) Do a minimum of 2 or 3 imagery exercises a week.
o) Have students develop vocabulary lists of imagery terms and concepts.
p) Encourage students to image with their parents. Give them some suggestions on how.

CHAPTER FOUR

CPS-Imagery Exercises

"If one advances confidently in the direction of his dreams to
live the life he has imagined, he will meet with a success
unexpected in common hours."

Henry David Thoreau

In this Chapter there are twenty-nine creative problem solving exercises
designed to free the imagination while attempting to generate better
ideas for students' problems. The exercises are presented in random order.
Selection should be based on teacher-student interest. It is important
that students have some baseline experience, in the form of introductory
guided and non-guided imagery exercises prior to engaging in the CPS
higher level imagery. The success of the following exercises will depend
largely on how imagery was introduced to the class. If time was taken
to clearly discuss the image process (in the form of group discussion and
feedback sessions) and students were given an appropriate number of
introductory image experiences, the CPS exercises will be highly successful in demonstrating how to get better ideas.

One of the most important aspects of the CPS-Imagery approach is
the successful creation of the Student Workshop. Be sure that the workshop guided image is administered carefully and effectively. It would be
a good idea for teachers to first experiment with the Workshop Image
with family and friends, in order to acquire the necessary rhythm, voice
quality and pausing. If you are not comfortable with the process, it's
better to wait until you have experienced imagery in as many different
modes as possible. Don't rush it! For some students it takes a little while
for them to be comfortable with imagination-type images, which are the
basic CPS exercises. Therefore, it's best to begin exposing students to
imagery through the use of reality-type images, e.g., images of nature,
images of familiar things, places, people, etc. Imagery is a wonderful
natural process that needs to be handled like an Art, and as with all art,

you cannot rush it.

Be sure that you have sufficient time when administering a CPS exercise. Determine how much time you need for : a) discussing the procedures for a particular exercise, b) administering the guided instructions and c) exercise follow-up, either Idea Workbook or imagery discussion. Remember, the time spent on the Idea Workbook may be just as valuable as the image exercise. So don't ignore the written part of the creative problem solving process. It is through the writing and conceptualizing part of the process where ideas are scrutinized and put into a plan of action.

Can I Change The Imagery Exercises Instructions?

By all means! It's what makes imagery so effective and so personal. Get familiar with the phraseology first, then feel free to modify any image suggestion or Idea Workbook activity. The options presented which each exercise are solely for the purpose of encouraging the personalizing of the images. Have the students suggest ways of modifying the various exercises. Growth in imagery occurs best, when both teacher and student work openly and cooperatively to improve the process.

If you have not thoroughly read Chapter 3, please go back and do so. You should not begin the CPS-Imagery exercises until you have done the following:

a)   Read Chapters 1, 2, and 3 of Using Imagery In Creative Problem Solving
b)   Administered several introductory imagery exercises (guided and non-guided)
c)   Conducted several group discussion sessions on the nature of imagery and how it works
d)   Practiced the Workshop Image with family and friends
e)   Secured Idea Workbooks for all students in the class
f)   Thoroughly discussed Terms and Concepts outlined in Chapter 3

It also would be very advantageous to have read *200 Ways of Using Imagery In The Classroom*, Bagley & Hess, 1982, prior to engaging in CPS imagery work.

HOW THE PROCESS WORKS

The following CPS-Imagery Exercises can be used with students in grades 4 to 12. The exercises ranging from 5 to 20 minutes can be presented to the entire class, a small group or even on an individual basis. The major purpose of the technique is to allow students the opportunity to a) look at their problems in a strange and different manner, b) make numerous mental manipulations and observations of the problem, c) be in a relaxed frame of mind for problem solving, d) experience the creative process through Imagination Imagery, and e) learn the nature and operations for balancing imagination and logical processes.

INSTRUCTIONS FOR CPS-EXERCISES

Step 1: Select an appropriate time where interruptions will be at a minimum

Step 2: Be sure the students have removed all books, etc., from their desks

Step 3: Give the students a brief introduction of the CPS exercise

Step 4: Ask the students to decide on a Target Problem (TP) for this exercise

Step 5: Give the students an idea of the approximate time (length) of the exercise.

Step 6: Remind the students not to talk or make any sounds during the exercise as it will disrupt the concentration of the group.

Step 7: Begin the exercise—reading the guided instructions

Note: Be sure to pause at appropriate moments—use voice inflections when necessary—feel free to change any of the statements and most importantly . . . be relaxed!

Step 8: Ask the students to write their responses to the experience in the CPS-Imagery Idea Workbook. Be sure to tell them how much time they have for this workbook activity.

Step 9: Option: At this point you can either move on to a new activity or you may wish to discuss the exercise with the group. Remember, never ask a student to share his/her experience

Remind the students that these CPS exercises don't guarantee a solution to a particular problem nor that each student will receive creative ideas each and every time. For some students the exercise can be very productive, for others, it could be a disappointment. Not all exercises will be liked by all students. In the same manner, not all imagery experiences are liked by all students. Imagery is a very personal experience. Therefore, expect a diversified reaction to each and every encounter with imagery.

The CPS exercises represent a high level, advanced form of imagery. It will take practice and time to become relaxed and confident with the process. Keep in mind that this imagery process of solution finding may be one of the *most valuable* experiences your students will ever have in school.

TITLE: ALTERNATE TIME-PAST

SUGGESTED TIME: 5 MINS

DESCRIPTION:
Prior to the start of the exercise the imager decides on a specific period of the past, e.g., revolutionary, or colonial, etc., which will serve as the setting and stimulus for image production. The imager should take a few minutes and just think about that specific time period—getting into the theme-traditions and experiences. The TP (Target Problem) is then selected. The exercise begins—the imager sees his/her TP actually taking place during the past. Let the customs, practices, beliefs, objects, things and events of the past interact with, and blend into your TP. Just let the content of your TP blend into the past.

GUIDED INSTRUCTIONS:
— Find a comfortable position, relax and begin focusing on your breathing
— Allow your self now . . . to enter your workshop
— Take a moment and sense your surroundings P = 30 sec.
— See yourself sitting comfortably in your Viewing Chair
IMAGE SET
— See all aspects of your TP taking place during a specific time period of the past
— In an effortless manner just let the images flow onto your screen.
— Take a few moments now and let it happen P = 3 mins.
— Alright . . . let the images of the past fade-out
— You have now finished the exercise
— Prepare to leave your workshop
— When I count to ten you will be back in your original setting
— One . . . ten wide awake.

OPTIONS:
a) Select a specific time for the entire class
b) Use appropriate background music for the designated period
c) Have students outline the specific events or situations relating to TP that they are interested in projecting in the past
d) Use two or more time periods during exercise

SUGGESTIONS FOR CPS-IMAGERY IDEA WORKBOOK
a)   Write a short story, newspaper article about the experience
b)   Describe how it was different from today
c)   What insight did you get from the experience?

TITLE: SUPER SLOW MOTION

SUGGESTED TIME: 10 MINS

DESCRIPTION:
In this exercise all image projection is in super slow motion. Each phase of TP will be seen in a very slow moving fashion. As with all exercise projections, images can be stilled and scanned. The instructor will designate the length of time for this particular exercise, start it, and conclude the procedure. It is important that the imager be instructed and reminded to concentrate on running the projection of objects and events of TP in super slow motion. Imager can select a segment of TP to be viewed or s/he may make a choice to project all aspects of TP.

GUIDED INSTRUCTIONS:
— Find a comfortable position, relax, and begin focusing on your breathing
— Allow yourself now to enter your workshop
— Take a moment and sense your surroundings P = 30
— See yourself sitting comfortably in your Viewing Chair
IMAGE SET
— Select your TP now and begin your image projection using your super slow motion ability
— Very slowly ..... let your images move P = 2 mins
— Continue your super slow motion easy and effortlessly P = 5 mins
— Alright, slowly allow your image to fade out
— You have now finished the exercise
— Prepare to leave your workshop
— When I count to ten you will be back in your original setting
— One ... ten wide awake

EXERCISE OPTIONS:
a) Use lost time for image projection
b) Use background music which has a slow motion rhythm
c) Use two or three levels of slow motion alternating between them as images are projected
d) Repeat a specific image running it over and over again in slow motion

SUGGESTIONS FOR CPS-IMAGERY IDEA BOOK

a) Describe your reaction to maintaining slow motion imagery throughout the exercise

b) List some suggestions for mastering the art of slow motion projection

c) Describe just how meanings (thoughts, ideas) entered your conscious awareness

d) Make a list of other areas where slow motion imagery would be valuable.

TITLE: WISE PERSON

SUGGESTED TIME: 20 MINS

DESCRIPTION:
This exercise involves guiding the imager up a mountain to meet a wise person and then down the mountain. The wise person will offer three positive suggestions relating to the imager's Target Problem. The instructor should use *Angels of Comfort* as background music as it is most appropriate for this particular guided image. This exercise should also be looked at, as a self-image motivation experience. It is a beautiful exercise which really should be used no more than twice in any one semester or school year. If you cannot obtain Angels of Comfort perhaps you can use some other New Age music selection.

GUIDED INSTRUCTIONS:
— Find a comfortable position, relax and begin to focus on your breathing
— Allow yourself now . . . to enter your workshop
— See yourself sitting comfortably in your Viewing Chair
IMAGE SET
— In the distance you see a large mountain and you are slowly walking toward this magnificent site.
    — It is a beautiful day — you see everything so clearly and you have lots of time.
— You continue walking and as you do you begin to realize just how immense this mountain is
— You are now reaching the base of the mountain
— Ahead of you is a special path — it has been created for you.
— Walk toward the path . . . slowly and safely
— You now begin your upward climb
— Feel the path under your feet
— Sense the ground as you climb
— You begin to feel a special awareness, a special sense of being
— Take a moment and observe all of nature P = 30 sec
— Notice how far into the distance you can see
— Take a deep breath . . . smelling the freshness of the air
— Listen to sounds of silence
— You continue to climb effortlessly

— You are reaching a level just below the clouds
— You begin to sense a great appreciation for the beauty and tranquility of nature
— You slowly begin to penetrate and move through a soft cloud mass
— Now you are above the clouds . . . climbing higher and higher
— You are more determined and feel extra strength
— You are now approaching a magnificent stairway
— You see the richness . . . colors and uniqueness of this stairway
— Slowly start your climb . . . up . . . up the stairway
— You now have reached the top of the mountain feeling a great sense of accomplishment
— Ahead of you . . . in the distance you see . . . sitting in a chair a Wise Person
— See this person clearly . . . with great detail
— Now listen as the Wise Person speaks to you P = 30 sec
— Alright, turn and begin your trip down the mountain
— As you walk away you sense a more positive self
— A detachment from negativity . . . a new outlook on life
— You feel energized and spirited
— See yourself walking down the stairway
— You've approached the cloud mass
— You just feel so at peace, so relaxed, and so positive
— Continue your slow descent
— You now begin to see the ground below
— In a moment you will reach the base of the mountain
— Alright, you have reached the end of your journey
— Leave the mountain area and take with you all of the positive images
— You have now finished the exercise
— Prepare to leave your workshop
— When I count to ten you will be back in your original setting
— One . . . ten, wide awake

OPTIONS:
a) Use an alternate setting such as desert, forest, lake, etc.
b) Use different background music
c) Let the Wise Person give the imager something else other than 3 positives
d) Shorten the time allowed for the exercise

CPS-IMAGERY IDEA WORKBOOK

a) Write about your entire journey
b) Write about "My Most Exciting Moment"
c) Discuss how the 3 positives relate to your TP
d) Describe your most powerful image
e) Describe in detail what the Wise Person looked like.

TITLE: MESSAGE FROM THE SEA

SUGGESTED TIME: 5 MINS

DESCRIPTION:
The exercise begins by having the imager see him/herself standing on a beach looking out toward the ocean. After a period of sensing this environment and feeling the relaxing effect, the imager then begins to anticipate a special bottle carrying an important message to slowly wash-up onto the shore. The bottle is opened, the message which is written on a note paper is read. During the exercise the sounds of ocean waves should be played as background (see New Age Select Music List).

GUIDED INSTRUCTIONS:
— Find a comfortable position, relax and begin focusing on your breathing
— Allow yourself now . . . to enter your workshop
— Take a moment and sense your surroundings P = 30
— See yourself sitting comfortably in your Viewing Chair
IMAGE SET
— Begin (ocean sounds) background
— You're standing on a beautiful beach
— Feel the sand under your feet and between your toes
— Listen to the sound of waves breaking in the distance
— Smell the salt in the ocean air
— Find a comfortable seat and begin anticipating the arrival of a special bottle, which is going to be washed ashore by the rolling waves
— Just allow all your concentration to focus out toward the sea P = 30
— And now . . . you begin to see . . . way in the distance a bottle . . . floating . . . floating
— You get up and walk to the water's edge
— Each wave brings the bottle closer
— You begin to see it . . . clearly
— Finally it's within your reach
— Slowly — pick it up
— Begin to remove the special note within the bottle
— Now focus all your attention as you begin to read this message
— Alright, prepare to leave the beach
— You have now finished the exercise
— You're in the workshop about to return to your original setting

— When I count to ten you will be back in your original setting
— One . . . ten wide awake.

OPTIONS:
a) Use a stream, lake, river, etc.
b) Instead of standing on a sea shore, imager could be in a boat
c) The imager could find something else in the bottle besides a message
d) It could be designed as non-guided-letting the imager create the action
e) There could be a few bottles with different messages

CPS-IMAGERY IDEA WORKSHOP
a) Describe the bottle in detail
b) Create a story on how the bottle got into the sea . . .
c) Relate message to TP
d) Describe ISM response while standing on beach

TITLE: PLUS-MINUS-INTERESTING

SUGGESTED TIME: 15 MINS

DESCRIPTION:

Prior to starting the exercise the imager decides on Target Problem. Then the imager will be instructed to image several possible solutions focusing approximately 60 seconds on each projected solution. At the end of solution projection (60 seconds), the imager will give the solution a title, enter it in the idea workbook and respond to the plus-minus and interesting feature of that particular solution. After this is completed the imager immediately goes to the workshop and prepares for the next 60 sec. solution projection. The same procedure is followed for as many different solutions as the imager cares to make. When the exercise is completed the imager should analyze all the written responses entered into the idea workbook.

IMAGERY EXERCISE GUIDED INSTRUCTIONS:

— Find a comfortable position, relax and begin focusing on your breathing
— Allow yourself now . . . to enter your workshop
— Take a moment and sense your surroundings P = 30 sec.
— See yourself sitting comfortably in your Viewing Chair
IMAGE SET
— You have 60 seconds to project solution to your TP - begin P = 60 sec
— Stop — now evaluate your solution ISM in terms of its plus-minus-and interesting features — record this information in your idea workbook (allow 3 mins for writing assignment)
— Alright back to your workshop P = 15 sec
IMAGE SET
Solution # 2
— Projection . . . you have 60 sec which is lots of time
— Begin — P = 60 sec
— Stop . . . evaluate ISM. Use idea workbook again
— Repeat procedure at least 3 times
— You have now finished the exercise
— Prepare to leave the workshop
— When I count to ten you will be back in your original setting
— One ...ten , wide awake

OPTIONS:
a)   Project solutions for longer periods of time
b)   Use other criteria for evaluating each solution
c)   Stay in workshop until all solutions are projected then do the evaluating all at once
d)   imager corner

CPS-IMAGERY FOR WORKBOOK
a)   Decide which solution has the most pluses and interesting features and lowest minus features. Write about the strengths of this solution which you think are the best
b)   Describe how each solution surfaced and came to your awareness
c)   Describe how the solutions were different
d)   What ideas did you get from this exercise. Tell about them

TITLE: TRANSFORMATION

SUGGESTED TIME: 5 MINS

DESCRIPTION:

The imager will be instructed to project Target Problem related images and at randomly selected intervals there will be a command of "Transform." At that instant, the imager will automatically select some object, event, situation or person relating to TP and transform or change its size, shape, color, movement etc., so that it will create an unusual or different association with the rest of the image content or image whole. After a period of integration, the imager will move on with regular TP image production and listen for the next transformation request. The transformation request should be at least 30 to 60 seconds apart. There should be a minimum of five such commands. Let the imagers transform whatever they like.

GUIDED INSTRUCTIONS

— Find a comfortable position, relax, and begin focusing on your breathing
— Allow yourself now to enter your workshop
— Take a moment and sense your surroundings P = 30 sec
— See yourself sitting comfortably in your Viewing Chair.
IMAGE SET
— Begin now . . . allowing images of your TP to flow onto the screen P = 30 sec
— At the command I will ask you to transform — completely change one of the objects, events, situations, or persons of your TP — you then let that new image creation interact with your basic image content
— Continue with TP projection P = 30 sec
TRANSFORM P = 15 sec
TRANSFORM P = 30 sec
TRANSFORM P = 30 sec
TRANSFORM P = 45 sec
TRANSFORM P = 10 sec
REPEAT PROCEDURE MORE IF YOU LIKE
— Alright, you have now completed this exercise
— Prepare to leave your workshop

— When I count to ten you will be back on your original setting
— One ... ten, wide awake

CPS-IMAGERY EXERCISE OPTIONS:
a) Let the imager direct the transformation signal
b) Use the same length of time in between pauses
c) Use repeated transformation with only one select feature TP image
d) Create a music piece which has a dramatic shift in tone at certain intervals which will serve as the signal to transform

SUGGESTIONS FOR CPS-IMAGERY IDEA WORKBOOK:
a) Describe how and what was transformed during exercises
b) Describe how the transformation influenced change in ISM formation
c) How might image transformation be used with life events? Explain
d) How might this exercise be used in a more non-guided approach? Explain

TITLE: DIRECT ANALOGY ANIMALS

SUGGESTED TIME: 8 MINS

DESCRIPTION:
In this exercise the imager will select a Target Problem and then have
the entire image content enacted through a select animal type of the
imager's choice. Everything about the TP will be viewed as being performed by animals. The imager will make a direct relationship between
his/her problem situation and an exact or parallel situation in the animal
world (For example if the real life problem deals with the lack of communication between two people—the imager will create the SAME lack of
communication situations between two animals). The entire problem
will be role-played by animals. The imager becomes an observer and just
allows the animals to act out each aspect of the TP.

GUIDED INSTRUCTIONS:
— Find a comfortable position, relax, and begin focusing on your breath-
   ing
— Allow yourself now . . . to enter your workshop
— Take a moment and sense your surroundings P = 30 sec
— See yourself sitting comfortably in your Viewing Chair.
IMAGE SET
— You have selected your TP . . . now allow every facet, every aspect of
   that situation to be seen, enacted by the animal of your choice.
— You will have five minutes . . . begin P = 5 mins
USE NATURE SOUNDS AS BACKGROUND (see Music Select Reference List)
— Alright . . . allow your images to fade-out
— You have completed this exercise
— Prepare to leave the workshop
— When I count to ten you will be back in your original setting
— One . . . ten, wide awake

OPTIONS:
a)   Use different species of animals
b)   Focus on only one aspect of TP having animals enact it in repeated
     images
c)   Make recording of real-life animal sounds and use as background

d) Make a list of the situations you would like to image (via animal direct analogy) prior to beginning the exercise

SUGGESTIONS FOR CPS-IDEA WORKBOOK:
a) Write about the most unusual aspect of this exercise
b) Create and write a cartoon of your leading character
c) Discuss how our solutions are different from the animal's solutions

TITLE: TEN FAMOUS PEOPLE

SUGGESTED TIME: 15 MINS

DESCRIPTION:
Prior to the start of the exercise the imager should make a list of the ten famous persons s/he would like to see involved in the discussion and solution of the target problem. Allow imager complete freedom in the selection process. ALL persons are acceptable. The exercise begins by focusing on the facial features of each person while they sit in a circle in the workshop (optional setting O.K.). Next, the imager will listen to the group as they discuss imager's TP (5 mins). Finally, imager listens, very intently as each famous person offers suggestions for solving the problem (5 - 10 mins).

GUIDED INSTRUCTIONS:
— Find a comfortable position, relax and begin focusing on your breathing
— Allow yourself now . . . to enter your workshop
— Take a moment and sense your surroundings P = 30 sec
— See yourself sitting comfortably in your Viewing Chair
IMAGE SET
— Establish a setting where you see very clearly your ten famous people
— Take a moment and focus in on each person's face seeing every detail and feature — do this one person at a time P = 2 mins
— Alright, now just sit back, relax and listen as your famous people discuss your TP P = 5 mins
— Alright, it is now time for each famous person to offer some suggestions on how you might solve your problem
— Again sit back, get comfortable and relax P = 5 min
— Alright, see yourself shaking hands and thanking with each person as they leave
— You have now finished the exercise
— Prepare to leave your workshop
— When I count to ten you will be back in your original setting
— One . . . ten, wide awake.

OPTIONS:
a)   Have less famous persons

b)   Have a certain type of famous person such as world leaders, artists, scholars, entertainers, etc.
c)   Have the famous people work on the TP differently, i.e., have them analyze it a certain way.
d)   Mix up the famous people, e.g., 5 from ancient times, 5 from the present.

SUGGESTIONS FOR CPS-IMAGERY IDEA WORKBOOK:
a)   Write about each person's contribution to the problem, their personal uniqueness and physical description
b)   Write about the unique features of this exercise
c)   How else could this exercise be used?
d)   Discuss how and why you would bring the people back again.

TITLE: FREE ASSOCIATION WORDS

SUGGESTED TIME: 10 MINS

CPS-IMAGERY EXERCISE DESCRIPTION

The imager will use two viewing screens for this exercise. Screen 1 will be used for fade-in projection of words (at least 10) presented to imager by instructor. Screen 2 will be used for free association image projection. The words will be presented in intervals of 30 seconds. The imager will hear and see the word and will then allow these associations to happen. The ISM relating to TP will be projected on screen 2. There will be a period of 30 seconds after image projection. Then the imager will prepare for the next stimulus word. The stimulus words should be randomly selected by the teacher from some written source, e.g., text, catalog, newspaper etc.

GUIDED INSTRUCTIONS:

— Find a comfortable position, relax and begin focusing on your breathing
— Allow yourself now . . . to enter your workshop.
— Take a moment and sense your surroundings P = 30 sec
— See yourself sitting comfortably in your Viewing Chair
IMAGE SET
— Begin by creating two large screens
— See them clearly . . . in detail
— Now focus on screen 1
— When you hear the stimulus word . . . allow the word to fade in on screen 1 — then have it fade out as your attention shifts to screen 2 where you will just allow images to appear, triggered by the stimulus word related to your TP
— You will have 30 seconds in between word presentations
— Relax P = 10 sec
IMAGE SET
— Word 1   P30
— Word 2   P30
— Word 3   P30
— Word 4   P30
— Word 6   P30
— Word 7   P30

— Word 8	P30
— Word 9	P30
— Word 10	P30

— Alright you have now finished the exercise
— Prepare to leave your workshop
— When I count to ten you will be back in your original setting
— One . . . ten, wide awake

OPTIONS:

a) Use different methods for word selection
b) Allow for longer imager projection time
c) Use only one screen
d) Allow imager to conjure up stimulus words
e) Use some type of categorization of words, e.g., action words, nature words, etc.

SUGGESTIONS FOR IMAGERY—IDEA WORKBOOK
a) List words and their associated ISMs
b) List 3 most important associations made during exercises
c) Describe the progression or degree of ISM response

TITLE: IMAGE REPETITION

SUGGESTED TIME: 5 MINS

DESCRIPTION:

In this exercise the use of repeated images will be the major CPS approach. The imager will select the image content from the Target Problem. The specific content will then be repeated several times through short image projection. The instructor will announce the start and end of each repeated image. A minimum of five repetitions should be used, more if interest is high. The imager may stay with one specific image during repetition or can just allow related images to flow onto screen. Regardless of content selection imager will automatically receive new and different perspectives for each repeated image.

GUIDED INSTRUCTIONS:

— Find a comfortable position, relax and begin focusing on your breathing
— Allow yourself now . . . to enter your workshop.
— Take a moment and sense your surroundings P = 30 sec
— See yourself sitting comfortably in your Viewing Chair
IMAGE SET
— You will have 30 sec to image your TP — which is lots of time

   1 Ready — begin P = 30 sec
      Stop — clear screen
      Relax P = 10 sec
   2 Ready — begin P = 30 sec
      Stop — clear screen
      Relax P = 10 sec
   3 Ready — begin P = 30 sec
      Stop — clear screen
      Relax P = 10 sec
   4 Ready — begin P = 30 sec
      Stop — clear screen
      Relax P = 10 sec
   5 Ready — begin P = 30
      Stop — clear screen
      Relax P = 10 sec
— You have now finished the exercise

— Prepare to leave your workshop
— When I count to ten you will be back in your original setting
— One ... ten, wide awake

OPTIONS:
a)   Allow for longer image projection
b)   Do several more image repetitions
c)   Come out of workshop after each image repetition in order to record ISM response
d)   Use fade-in, fade-out instructions
e)   Allow imager to do repeated images according to their own time schedule

SUGGESTIONS FOR CPS-IMAGERY IDEA WORKBOOK
a)   Record ISM response for each image repetition
b)   Make a list of new perspectives, attained during repeated images
c)   Describe experience in terms of (1) image progression (2) image depth (3) image shifting
d)   Write about "my most powerful image "

TITLE: CHANGING COLORS

SUGGESTED TIME: 10 MINS

DESCRIPTION:

In this exercise the imager will project Target Problem images using a range of different colors. The imager will be instructed to change colors, to see everything within the image content in a specified color. When the instructor announces the color the imager begins immediately seeing every facet, every detail of the image in the prescribed color. When the next color is announced, the imager makes the appropriate color transformation. After several announced colors the imager will integrate colors of his/her choice. The color transformations can be applied to any aspect of TP.

GUIDED INSTRUCTIONS:

— Find a comfortable position, relax and begin focusing on your breathing
— Allow yourself now . . . to enter your workshop
— Take a moment and sense your surroundings
— You're now comfortably sitting in your Viewing Chair
IMAGE SET
— Begin focusing on one aspect of TP P = 30 sec
— Let us begin with our first color transformation
— Slowly . . . begin to see everything in your TP in the color green . . . P = 30 sec
— Now see everything in the color orange P = 30
— Now see everything in the color yellow P = 30
— Now . . . blue . . . P = 30
— Alright, . . . I want you to continue making color transformations on your own
— Take a few minutes and use any color you would like
— Alright . . . you have finished the exercise
— Fade out all images and prepare to leave the workshop
— When I count to ten you will be back in your original setting
— One . . . . ten, wide awake

OPTIONS:

a)   Use two colors during all image projections

b)   Use multi-color combinations
c)   Use creative coloring (mixtures, shades, textures, etc.)
d)   Use only one color throughout the exercise, however allow the color to evolve into many tones, shades and degrees of intensity

SUGGESTIONS FOR CPS-IMAGERY IDEA WORKBOOK
a)   List color and corresponding ISM responses
b)   Describe how the color transformations changed your perspective about the image
c)   Describe any differences between being told the color and projecting colors of your own choice
d)   Discuss any unusual or funny reactions caused by the color transformations

TITLE: OTHER CULTURE

SUGGESTED TIME: 10 MINS

DESCRIPTION:
The imager will select a familiar culture and then have people from that culture act out the Target Problem. The imager needs to select appropriate and similar situations so that the Target Problem is seen as realistically as possible, e.g., similar ages, family composition, living conditions, environmental surroundings, etc. Allow the imager some pre-exercise time to organize and plan the situations that will be transferred to another culture. Decide which aspect of the Target Problem will be transferred and projected through images.

GUIDED INSTRUCTIONS:
— Find a comfortable position, relax . . . and begin focusing on your breathing
— Allow yourself now . . . to enter your workshop
— Take a moment and sense your surroundings
— You're sitting comfortably in your Viewing Chair
IMAGE SET
— You have already selected your other culture
— Allow your TP to be acted out by people from another culture . . .
just let all the circumstances of your Target Problem transfer into the lives and events of a completely different culture.
— Just watch any aspect of your problem being experienced by these people . . . see it as a reality . . . begin. You have lots of time P = 5 mins.
— Alright, allow your images to fade away
— Complete the exercise and slowly begin to prepare to leave the workshop
— When I count to ten you will be back in your original setting
— One . . . ten, wide awake

OPTIONS
a) Suggest a particular culture to be used for the exercise—all students use same culture
b) Select one aspect of TP and transfer it to several preselected cultures
c) Use double screen imagery techniques, screen 1 (TP in our culture)

screen 2 (TP being solved in other culture). Keep alternating between screens

d) Select several important aspects of TP and transfer it to other cultures

SUGGESTIONS FOR CPS-IMAGERY IDEA WORKBOOK
a) How was your TP different in another culture? Describe
b) Were personalities, attitudes of people different in other cultures? How? Describe
c) What was the most important thing you learned from this exercise?
d) If you used more than one culture, discuss how the cultures differed with respect to your Target Problem

TITLE: ABOVE THE EARTH

SUGGESTED TIME: 8 MINS

DESCRIPTION:
The imager will focus on Target Problem in the workshop and then will slowly begin to take-off into the sky in a large helium balloon. Their Target Problem will fade out as images of earth, sky and clouds come into focus. The imager is to shift concentration from the Target Problem to the above the earth experience. After several minutes of going through this above earth experience the imager is slowly brought back to earth— and upon return, will find a valuable solution to the Target Problem. This idea or solution will emerge as concentration is directed back to Target Problem.

GUIDED INSTRUCTIONS:
— Find a comfortable position, relax and begin focusing on your breathing
— Allow yourself now . . . to enter your workshop
— Take a moment and sense your surroundings
— You're sitting comfortably in your Viewing Chair
IMAGE SET
— Begin projecting your Target Problem onto your Viewing Screen
— Take a moment and just let the images flow onto your screen — Alright . . . slowly have your TP fade out. P = 15 sec
— You are now ready to climb into a large, safe, helium balloon.
— Just see yourself climbing in and preparing for a safe journey above the earth
— You're off . . . feel yourself slowly rising up . . . up
— Notice everything . . . P = 30 sec
— You're now high above the earth
— Continue experiencing all the sites, sense your new environment . . . the colors, sounds, etc.
— Continue your trip until the earth is a tiny dot P = 60 sec
— Feel your power . . . feel the peace . . . feel how focused you are . . . enjoy this moment. P = 60 sec
— Alright . . . slowly and safely begin to head down toward earth
— Begin to see the earth getting larger and larger as you continue your slow descent

— See yourself safely preparing to land
— You have landed . . . you're back
— Now slowly fade out this experience and return to your workshop
— Now focus your attention onto your Viewing Screen . . . in a moment you will receive a new idea, a solution to your Target Problem . . . relax and wait for it to come
— Alright you have your new idea!
— Have your images fade out and prepare to leave the workshop
— The exercise has ended
— When I count to ten you will be back in your original setting
— One . . . ten, wide awake

OPTIONS:

a) Do exercise with other types of vehicles, e.g., rocket, ship, magic carpet, plane, etc.
b) Visit another planet during the journey
c) Let the entire journey be non-guided
d) Suggest that there will be some new ideas concerning the Target Problem when the imager returns

SUGGESTIONS FOR CPS-IMAGERY IDEA WORKBOOK

a) Describe in detail your helium balloon
b) Write "stream of consciousness" style "I felt . . ."
c) Write about the new idea you received on your return to earth
d) Write about some interesting images seen during your outer space experience.

TITLE: MAGICAL SLIDE PROJECTION

SUGGESTED TIME: 8 MINS

DESCRIPTION:
While in the workshop the imager receives a special delivery. It is a marvelous new "Magical Slide Projector" which has the capability of projecting great new ideas on any subject. This new mechanical device has unlimited potential and is quite easy to use. You just sit back, hold on to the magical switch and just press for each new picture, image to come onto your Viewing Screen. Have the imager select a Target Problem to be used in this exercise. Once the Target Problem is selected turn on the magical slide projector and begin seeing new ideas, new images each time you press its special switch.

GUIDED INSTRUCTIONS:
— Find a comfortable position, relax ... and begin focusing on your breathing.
— Allow yourself now ... to enter your workshop
— make a moment and sense your surroundings P = 30 sec
— You're comfortably sitting in your Viewing Chair
IMAGE SET
— You are waiting for a special delivery of a marvelous new idea — finding machine called "magical slide projector"
— The delivery is now being made—see the arrival of this new amazing piece of equipment
— Set it up next to your Viewing Chair
— Now tell the magical slide projector the title or theme of your Target Problem
— Now grab the special switch, sit back, relax and prepare to receive new ideas each time you press the switch
— Ready — begin P = 3 mins
— Alright ... turn off the magical slide projector
— Put it safely away
— Prepare to leave the workshop
— The exercise has ended
— When I count to ten you will be back in your original setting
— One ... ten, wide awake

OPTIONS:

a) Create a different name for the new machine, and have it do other things as well, e.g., play music

b) Guide the imager through a series of pressing the switch, e.g., call out each new idea

c) Spend more time on acquainting the machine with imager's Target Problem, e.g., type into the machine all facts about the Target Problem.

d) Allow the magical slide projector to do some image manipulations, e.g., zoom-in, transform, scan, etc.

SUGGESTIONS FOR CPS-IMAGERY IDEA WORKBOOK

a) Describe what the magical slide projector looked like.

b) Make a list of possible new names for the machines

c) Make a list of all the ideas, images the projector delivered

d) Illustrate how you used the magical slide projector

TITLE: MYSTERY CAVE

SUGGESTED TIME: 10 MINS

DESCRIPTION:
The imager will take a journey through a cave. At different points along the journey the imager will discover a special clue relating to a great new idea that will emerge at the end of the cave. Each clue will be related to this new idea that will be discovered toward the end of the journey. The imager will discover these clues in whatever manner the imagination decides. All of the clues will relate to the "big new idea" which in turn will relate to the imager's Target Problem.

GUIDED INSTRUCTIONS:
— Find a comfortable position, relax and begin focusing on your breathing
— Allow yourself now . . . to enter your workshop
— Take a moment and sense your surroundings P = 30 sec
— You're sitting comfortably in your Viewing Chair
IMAGE SET (START MUSIC IF YOU HAVE AN APPROPRIATE SELECTION)
— You are coming to the base of a large mountain
— Find a special entrance which will lead you safely into the "mystery cave"
— Along the journey you are going to find, unusual places, very interesting clues relating to a big new idea for your Target Problem.
— Let your imagination discover these clues as you walk slowly through this mystery cave.
— Begin P = 3 mins
— Alright . . . you have now found several clues all relating to the big new idea.
— You now can see light ahead of you
— Move toward the light as it will lead you out of the cave and to the discovery of the big new idea P = 60 sec
— Alright . . . you have safely completed your journey through the mystery cave.
— Prepare to leave this exercise and return to your original setting
— When I count to ten you will be back
— One . . . ten, wide awake.

OPTIONS:

a) Use more descriptors in guiding imager through the cave, e.g., being more specific
b) Announce the clue discoveries according to the tempo of the background music
c) Instead of a cave, use a path in a forest, a jungle etc.
d) Take some people with you, e.g., friends, family etc.

SUGGESTIONS FOR CPS-IMAGERY IDEA WORKBOOK

a) Draw and write about all the clues discovered in the journey
b) Describe all the unusual events that were imaged during the journey
c) Describe how the big idea came to you
d) What effect did the music (if used) have on the experience?

TITLE: TEXTURE BONANZA

SUGGESTED TIME: 15 MINS

DESCRIPTION:

In this exercise the imager will experience a wide range of textures as he/she walks through a beautiful meadow. Some of the textures will be announced by the instructor, other textures will be experienced by the imager in a spontaneous manner. The textures will unlock ideas relating to the imager's Target Problem. These ideas will come in a spontaneous manner. Each texture should be totally experienced (touch, smell, size, shape, colors, etc.).

GUIDED INSTRUCTIONS

— Find a comfortable position, relax . . . and begin focusing on your chair breathing
— Allow yourself now to enter your workshop
— Take a moment and sense your surroundings P = 30 sec
— You're sitting comfortably in your Viewing Chair
IMAGE SET
— I want you to imagine yourself walking through a beautiful meadow on a clear sunny day
— Observe all of nature P = 30 sec
— You are going to experience many different textures in the next few moments—these textures will trigger some new ideas
— Don't look for the ideas — just experience each texture to its fullest
— Alright — let us begin with the texture of sponge
— See and feel everything as spongey P = 60 sec
— Next, see and feel everything as cotton P = 60 sec
— Next, see and feel everything as sandy P = 60 sec
— Next, see and feel everything as wet P = 60 sec
— Alright . . . I want you to now direct your own texture experiences . . . begin P = 3 mins
— Alright . . . finish this last texture experience and slowly leave the meadow area P = 30 sec
— The exercise has ended, prepare to return to your original setting
— When I count to ten you will be back
— One . . . ten, wide awake

OPTIONS:
a) Change the setting, use a park, the country, an island etc.
b) Guide a few texture experiences with specific sensory instructions, e.g., "feel," "smell," etc.
c) Use background music with changing tempos for each texture—let the music guide the imager through the texture experience
d) Go indoors with the exercise and experience the textures in the workshop

SUGGESTIONS FOR IMAGERY IDEA WORKBOOK
a) List the ideas and feelings received from each of the textures
b) Draw each texture
c) Make a list of descriptions for each texture
d) Which texture provided you the biggest sensory experience? Why?

TITLE: TRAIN TO NOWHERE

SUGGESTED TIME: 15 MINS

DESCRIPTION:
In this exercise the imager gets in a train and goes on a long journey to nowhere. The exercise is directed by the imager. Along the route the imager will spontaneously see large "message billboards" that will have significant information concerning the imager's Target Problem. The imager will have complete freedom to decide when and where these billboards will appear as well as the number that will appear.

GUIDED INSTRUCTIONS:
— Find a comfortable position, relax ... and begin focusing on your breathing
— Allow yourself now ... to enter your workshop
— Take a moment and sense your surroundings P = 30 sec
— You're sitting comfortably in your Viewing Chair
IMAGE SET
— You're at a train station about to board a magnificent train to nowhere.
— See yourself getting on the train to begin your journey
— Along the journey you will see many large message billboards with important information about your Target Problem
— Just let them appear wherever you wish
— Have a good trip ... P = 10 mins
  (This is a good exercise for background music, perhaps with a fast pace, up-beat.)
— Alright, have your train return P = 30 sec
— You're back, safe and full of information
— The exercise is over — prepare to leave your workshop and return to your original setting
— When I count to ten you will be back
— One ... ten, wide awake

OPTIONS:
a)   Instead of a train use a car, bus, boat, etc.
b)   Instead of message billboards, use signs on buildings, signs on windows, on flags, etc.
c)   Make the exercise more guided (by instructing the imager when

and where to see the important messages)

d)   Have the train stop at different locations. Have people get on with messages (written on paper, in a newspaper, a note, etc.) for the imager. Each person will come over to the imager and present a message in a different format

SUGGESTIONS FOR CPS IDEA WORKBOOK

a)   Describe where the train to nowhere took you
b)   Write about each important billboard/message
c)   Illustrate through drawings what the train looked like
d)   Discuss the most important message. Tell why this message was a superior one

TITLE: CHANGING IDENTITIES

SUGGESTED TIME: 10 MINS

DESCRIPTION:

In this exercise the imager will alternate between different personalities. The imager will decide which persons to become as the Target Problem is being projected. The imager will emerge into each person's identity and act according to how that person identifies with the Target Problem. The imager will totally assume that person's identity, see things as that person would, react as that person would, make decisions as that person would. Each time the imager becomes a different person the Target Problem should be repeated (or whatever aspect of TP is being projected). Remember, the key is to see things from the "eyes" of the new person (new identity). (Make sure the imager understands this exercise before beginning.)

GUIDED INSTRUCTIONS

— Find a comfortable position, relax and begin focusing on your breathing
— Allow yourself now . . . to enter your workshop
— Take a moment and sense your surroundings P = 30 sec
— You're sitting comfortably in your Viewing Chair
IMAGE SET
— You are going to have the opportunity of experiencing your Target Problem from other people's points of view
— Focus now on your TP
— Now just feel yourself changing into this other person — do this however you feel most comfortable
— Now let your TP continue only now you are a different person . . . thinking and acting only as this other person would P = 2 mins
— Alright — it's time to change
— Slowly become a different person . . . again thinking and acting as this person would act P = 2 mins
— Alright . . . one more change . . . begin P = 2 mins
— Good . . . you have now seen your Target Problem from the eyes of three different people P = 15 sec
— Bring the exercise to a close P = 15 sec
— When I count to ten you will be back in your original setting
— One . . . ten . . . wide awake

OPTIONS:
a) Select only one different personality and view several Target Problems
b) Change the length of time for image projection
c) Involve only family members in this exercise (seeing the Target Problem only as the different family members would)
d) Alternate between different settings, i.e., have the TP take place in different locations

SUGGESTIONS FOR CPS IDEA WORKBOOK
a) Describe how each person reacted to Target Problem
b) Which new identity was the easiest to assume? Why?
c) Describe the strangest thing about this exercise
d) Make a list of all the new thoughts that came to mind during exercise

TITLE: ODORS FROM NATURE

SUGGESTED TIME: 8 MINS

DESCRIPTION:

In this exercise the imager will experience a variety of pleasant nature odors while walking in the woods. The imager will be totally engulfed in the odors' essences. Each odor will produce a new idea relating to the Target Problem. The instructor will guide the imager in and out of the odor experiences. Each odor will be presented for one minute. (Use music with nature sounds.)

GUIDED INSTRUCTIONS:

— Find a comfortable position, relax, and begin focusing on your breathing
— Allow yourself now . . . to enter your workshop
— Take a moment and sense your surroundings
— You're sitting comfortably in your Viewing Chair
IMAGE SET
— You're walking into a beautiful woods on a magnificently clear, warm, day
— In a moment you are going to experience many beautiful nature odors
— Allow yourself to be totally engulfed by these radiant smells
— At the end of each odor you are going to receive a new idea for a Target Problem
— Let us begin
— First, allow the odor of pine to come into your awareness — P = 60 sec
— Next, let the odor of a magnificent rose come into your awareness — P = 60 secs
— Next, you're standing alongside some huge apple trees . . . just sense the odor - P = 60 sec
— As you walk along . . . notice some strawberry bushes. Allow this fresh natural odor to engulf you.
— Continue your walk and allow other odors to come into your being P = 2 mins
— Alright, slowly leave this beautiful woods P = 15 sec
— Take with you all the wonderful images
— The exercise is over. When I count to ten you will be back in your original setting
One . . . ten, wide awake.   **87**

OPTIONS:
a)   Allow longer or shorter periods of time to experience each odor
b)   Focus in on one thing of nature and let all the odors come from that
c)   Use "New Age" music with nature sounds as background
d)   Use different settings to experience the odors, e.g., change countries, climates, etc.

SUGGESTIONS FOR CPS-IMAGERY IDEA WORKBOOK
a)   Describe each odor in full detail
b)   Discuss how the odor engulfed you. Be specific.
c)   Make a list of other odors you could experience in this manner
d)   Make a list of ideas gotten from each individual odor.

TITLE: RAINBOW RAY

SUGGESTED TIME: 15 MINS

DESCRIPTION:
In this beautiful guided experience the imager will float up into the sky and slowly enter six levels of a magnificent rainbow. The levels are: level 1 - tranquility, level 2- harmony, level 3- love, level 4 - trust, level 5 - potential and level 6 - peace. As the imager is guided through the levels s/he will experience different colors for each level. Each level and its corresponding color will provide the imager with some new ideas relating to the Target Problem. This will happen naturally as the experience deepens with concentration.

GUIDED INSTRUCTIONS:
— Find a comfortable position, relax ... and begin focusing on your breathing
— Allow yourself now to enter your workshop
— Take a moment and sense your surroundings P = 30 sec
— You're sitting comfortably in your Viewing Chair

IMAGE SET
— I want you to image that you are safely floating up into the air P = 10 sec
— Slowly you float upwards P = 15 sec
— Listen to the sounds of silence as you continue this peaceful journey
— Ahead of you is a magnificent multicolored rainbow

START MUSIC: (Suggested selection: RAINBOW MASTERS FROM SOURCE SAMPLER VOL. 1)
— You are going to float into the six levels of the rainbow
— Let us begin ... the first level is the level of tranquility ... totally sense it and see and feel its color P = 1 min
— Now slowly begin to move into the next level which is harmony ... again totally sense it and see and feel a new color P = 1 min
— Now the third level which is love ... move into and through the color of love P = 1 min
— Now into the level of trust P = 1 min
— Now into the fifth level which is potential P = 1 min
— Finally rise into the highest level ... the level of peace P = 1 min
— You are now at the very top of the rainbow ... totally relaxed and energized

89

— You feel strength and alertness, and have a greater sense of how to handle your problems
— Alright . . . take all these images and feelings with you as you begin to move slowly back down through the six levels of the rainbow
— Just feel yourself moving effortlessly through the rainbow
— Now you are coming safely back down to the ground
— You are safe and on the ground
— The exercise is over
— When I count to ten you will be back in your original setting
— One . . . ten, wide awake

OPTIONS:
a)   Announce a particular color for each level
b)   Change the names for each level of the rainbow or let the imager give it a name as s/he goes through the rainbow
c)   Move through the rainbow levels in a vehicle, e.g., a balloon, a magical carpet, an airplane etc.
d)   Use additional descriptions with each rainbow level.

SUGGESTIONS FOR CPS-IMAGERY IDEA WORKBOOK
a)   Describe the feeling you got from each level of the rainbow
b)   Write about your favorite level of the rainbow
c)   Make up new and different names for each level of the rainbow
d)   List the new ideas you received from the different levels.

TITLE: FLOATING CLOUDS

SUGGESTED TIME: 8 MINS

DESCRIPTION:

After a relaxation in the Workshop, the imager will begin a series of floating cloud projections. The first few clouds will be announced by the instructor, after which, the imager will control the cloud projections. The clouds will float into the imager's awareness. Once the cloud becomes the object of relaxed concentration, a new idea or solution will emerge, concerning the imager's TP. Don't force the ideas—just wait for them to appear with each floating cloud.

GUIDED INSTRUCTIONS:

— Find a comfortable position, relax ... and begin focusing on your breathing
— Allow yourself now ... to enter your workshop
— Take a moment and sense your surroundings P = 30 sec
— You are now comfortably in your Viewing Chair

IMAGE SET

— In a moment you are going to experience a series of floating clouds. They will be appearing very slowly ... one-by-one
— Once the cloud is in front of you or in full focus, simply maintain relaxed attention
— With each cloud you are going to receive a new and different idea for your TP
— Alright, let us begin
— Imagine a clear, beautiful sky
— Now begin to see Cloud #1 slowly coming into your picture P = 60 sec
— Fade-out P = 5 sec
— Now ... Cloud #2 P = 60 sec
— Fade-out P = 5 sec
— Now ... Cloud #3 P = 60 sec
— Fade-out P = 5 sec
— Alright ... take a few moments and continue having clouds float in and out of your view ... begin P = 3 mins
— Alright ... have your last cloud fade-out
— You have finished the exercise

— Prepare to leave the Workshop and return to your original setting
— When I count to ten you will be back
— One . . . ten, wide awake

OPTIONS:
a) Guide the imager to a specific location prior to seeing the clouds, e.g., an island, meadow, etc.
b) Allow the imager to direct all floating cloud projections
c) Use appropriate music to stimulate cloud images
d) Focus on just one cloud for an extended period of time, e.g., five mins

SUGGESTIONS FOR CPS-IMAGERY IDEA WORKBOOK:
a) Draw one or more clouds
b) Name and describe each of the clouds seen during the exercise
c) Describe how an idea emerged from the floating cloud
d) Make a list of all the ways you could use the sky, clouds, etc., for a similar CPS exercise.

TITLE: CARTOON CHARACTERS

SUGGESTED TIME: 8 MINS

DESCRIPTION:

In this exercise the imager selects several of his/her favorite cartoon characters who will assume different roles within the imager's Target Problem. The cartoon characters are brought into the TP at specified intervals and may be used in any manner. Allow the personality of each cartoon character to emerge in whatever role they may be assuming. Before you begin this exercise make sure you have decided what cartoon characters will be playing the various real-person roles.

GUIDED INSTRUCTIONS:

— Find a comfortable position, relax....and begin focusing on your breath-
  ing
— Allow yourself now . . . to enter your workshop
— Take a moment and sense your surroundings P = 30 sec
— You are sitting comfortably in your viewing chair
IMAGE SET
— Allow your first cartoon character to emerge onto your screen and
  slowly assume the identity of a real person associated with your Target
  Problem
— Have this cartoon character get involved with your TP
— Let the images flow naturally
— Notice the personality of this cartoon character
— Take a moment and just watch the cartoon character. . . P = 15 sec
— Alright . . . it's now time to bring in a second cartoon character . . .
  begin . . . just let it happen as you did with the first P = 1 min
— Now continue to bring in other cartoon characters until all your real
  people have new cartoon character identities
— Remember. . . let the characters act out all the dimensions of your TP
— Just observe as they deal with your TP P = 2 mins
— Alright, allow all the cartoon characters to leave . . . P = 10 sec
— The exercise is completed . . . slowly begin to leave the Workshop and
  return to your original setting . . . P = 10 sec
— When I count to ten you will be back
— one . . . ten, wide awake

OPTIONS:
a) Have the entire class use the same designated cartoon character
b) Select cartoon characters on the basis of a general descriptor, e.g., powerful, funny, speedy, etc.
c) Select a family of cartoon characters and let them act out your TP
d) Create a new cartoon character never before seen.

SUGGESTIONS FOR CPS-IMAGERY IDEA WORKBOOK:
a) How would one of your cartoon characters describe your TP?
b) List and describe the funny images you experienced during this exercise
c) How did the cartoon characters change your thinking about your TP? Explain
d) Create a new cartoon character with a unique personality.

TITLE: CHANGING CLIMATES

SUGGESTED TIME: 10 MINS

DESCRIPTION:
While focusing on the TP the imager will experience a series of climate changes. As the climate conditions are announced, the imager will begin projecting images of the TP occurring within the specific condition. Don't force the images . . . just allow them to flow onto the screen in whatever form they occur. First sense the new climate condition, then relate the TP to the new climate.

GUIDED INSTRUCTIONS:
— Find a comfortable position, relax, . . . and begin focusing on your breathing
— Allow yourself now . . . to enter your Workshop
— Take a moment and sense your surroundings P = 30 sec
— You are now sitting comfortably in your Viewing Chair
IMAGE SET
— Begin focusing on your Target Problem
— Just allow the images to flow onto your screen P = 30 sec
— Now I want you to get ready to experience several different climate conditions
— As the different conditions are presented, I want you to let your TP be seen under the new conditions
— Alright . . . Condition #1 . . . "A Winter Snow Storm" P = 45 sec
— Fade-out P = 5 sec
— Condition #2 . . . "A Very Hot and Dry Day" P = 45 sec
— Fade out P = 5 sec
— Condition #3 . . . "A Very Windy Day" P = 45 sec
— Fade-out P = 5 sec
— Condition #4 . . . "A Heavy Rain Storm" P = 45 sec
— Fade-out P = 5 sec
— Condition #5 . . . "A Cloudy Day" P = 45 sec
— Fade-out P = 5 sec
— Condition #6 Now create your own conditions for a few moments P = 2 mins
— Fade-out P = 10 sec

— Alright, slowly clear your screen and prepare to leave the Workshop
— When I count to ten you will be back in your original setting
— One ... ten wide awake

OPTIONS:
a) Use one climate condition and repeat it several times.
b) Use a specially prepared nature-sound tape with each changing weather condition, e.g., rain, winds, running water, etc.
c) Let all the different climate conditions be established by the imager
d) Use environmental setting changes to accompany the various climate changes.

SUGGESTIONS FOR CPS-IMAGERY IDEA WORKBOOK:
a) Describe how the TP changed during each climate condition.
b) Describe your somatic response (feelings) for each of the climate conditions
c) Write about "My Most Powerful Image"
d) Discuss why you think a particular climate condition (be specific) would be best for solving your TP

TITLE: REVERSE MOTION

SUGGESTED TIME: 5 MINS

DESCRIPTION:
This exercise requires the imager to focus on the best possible outcome (solution) for the TP. After seeing the solution for a minute or two, the imager is instructed to begin the process of reversing the projection. Allowing images to unfold to what happened just before the final outcome. What was the final step that brought the solution? And what happened just before that . . . and before that? Have the imager visualize each step of the solution's unfolding. Don't force the images...just wait and let them flow onto the workshop screen. The sequence and nature of the reverse image projections will be determined by the imager as will the duration of the projected images. The important thing is to have a final outcome, a best solution, first-then proceed with the reverse motion process. Be extra patient with this exercise.

GUIDED INSTRUCTIONS:
— Find a comfortable position, relax, and begin focusing on your breathing
— Allow yourself now to enter your workshop
— Take a moment and sense your surroundings P = 30 sec
— See yourself sitting comfortably in your Viewing Chair
IMAGE SET
— Image your TP totally solved
— Create and image clearly seeing the best possible outcome
— See all of its detail—its exactness—its completeness
— Now let us start the reverse motion process
— Turn your image projector to reverse position
— Very slowly see the event or situation that occurred right before the final outcome
— Next, again in reverse, see the next set of events or conditions
— Continue this procedure for a few moments
— Alright . . . stop now . . . I want you to switch your image projector to its forward position
— Begin to see in a connected, sequential manner all the images leading up to the final successful outcome

— Just sit back . . . relax, and allow the movie to run . . . P = 2 mins
  — Turn off the projector
  — Prepare to leave your workshop
  — When I count to ten you will be back at your original setting
  — One . . . ten . . . wide awake

OPTIONS:

a) Instead of a "running motion picture" have the imager focus on stills, frames or slides. The reverse process would be in the form of a series of pictures

b) Use a reverse forward procedure, going back then running the pictures in forward motion. Small segments of events or situations could be used

c) Use two or three final best outcomes or solutions. Make solutions different from each other

SUGGESTIONS FOR CPS-IMAGERY IDEA WORKBOOK:

a) Write a script for the reverse images highlighting and detailing the events as they unfold

b) Write ISM responses for each reverse segment of exercise

c) Draw and label any stills, frames, or slides

d) Make best idea list

TITLE: FANTASY-CPS

SUGGESTED TIME: 7 MINS

DESCRIPTION:

In this exercise the imager is encouraged to allow fantasy type images to interplay with TP. The emphasis is on evoking wild, unusual, and imaginative visualizations. The imager is directed to conjure-up different creative images while the TP-projection is maintained and scanned and manipulated, "See things in strange, funny ways". . . give items, objects, people, new identities, movements . . . remember the key to this exercise is to continually integrate the unusual with the reality TP content. Use the Workshop and Viewing Chair for this exercise. Don't force the images—direct them in an effortless manner. Be playful . . . you want to see things in strange ways. Take a few minutes before beginning these exercises and explain the basic theme and approach to be used.

GUIDED INSTRUCTIONS:
— Find a comfortable position, relax, and begin focusing on your breathing
— Allow yourself . . . now to enter your workshop
— Take a moment and sense your surroundings
— See yourself sitting comfortably in your Viewing Chair
IMAGE SET
— Begin seeing your TP in a strange, unusual way
— See things in new different colors
— Allow objects to move in strange ways
— Listen to funny sounds
— Now take a few minutes and creatively manipulate all dimensions of your TP P = 2 mins
— Alright . . . bring this exercise to a finish
— Prepare to leave the workshop
— When I count to ten, you will be back in your original setting
— One . . . ten . . . wide awake.

OPTIONS:
a) Allow less time for non-guided image projection giving more specific direction in creative manipulation through guided instructions

b) Create a "Fantasy Theme" and have the guided images follow it throughout the exercise
c) Create a "Fantasy Character" and have the character take a major role in the plot
d) Use image provoking music as background for the exercise, for example *Planets* by Tomita
e) Use a different setting for the exercise: a relaxing beach, country, mountains, etc.

SUGGESTIONS FOR CPS-IMAGERY IDEA WORKSHOP
a) Write out in detail all the creative images evoked during the exercise
b) Describe the most amazing feature of your exercise
c) Make a list of creative manipulations you would like to use during future Fantasy image projection
d) Make a list of new information obtained during exercise
e) Draw one or more of your creative images giving it a title, cartoon caption, etc.

TITLE: DOUBLE SCREEN

SUGGESTED TIME: 7 MINS

DESCRIPTION:
The imager creates two screens once in the workshop. Both screens must be clearly seen. The screens will be designated as Screen 1 and Screen 2. The imager will select a problem situation (Target Problem) and allow it to flow onto Screen 1, seeing it in actual, present circumstances. This projection will last 30 sec. Then the imager will turn-off Screen 1 projection and focus attention on Screen 2. On Screen 2 the imager will be instructed to see the target screen 2 projection. When Screen 2 projection has ended, the imager is to return to Screen 1 where the problem will be once again seen as it actually is. This procedure (alternating between Screen 1 and 2) should be repeated at least 3 times more if the imager is personally motivated by the exercise.

GUIDED INSTRUCTIONS:
— Find a comfortable position, relax and begin focusing on your breathing
— Allow yourself now to enter your workshop
— Take a moment and sense your surroundings P = 30 sec
— See yourself sitting comfortably in your viewing chair
IMAGE SET
— Begin by creating 2 large screens
— See them clearly . . . in detail
— Focus your attention on Screen 1
— Now take your previously identified target problem and allow it to be seen on Screen 1 . . . you have 30 sec — Lots of time
— Alright . . . now fade out screen 1 and turn your attention on screen 2
— See your target problem completely solved . . . you have 30 sec
— Turn off projection two and return to Screen 1 and again see your target problem as it actually is
— Repeat procedure at least three times
— You have now finished the exercise
— Prepare to leave your workshop
— When I count to ten you will be back in your original setting
— One . . . ten, wide awake

OPTIONS:

a) Allow for a longer image projection, e.g., 45 sec., 60 sec., etc.
b) Focus on more than one problem
c) Try three screens using screen 2 as transition screen
d) Use only one screen and use fade-in and fade-out technique
e) Discuss double screen exercise and suggest students do it on their own (non-guided)

SUGGESTIONS FOR CPS-IMAGERY IDEA WORKBOOK

a) Create two columns and write ISM response for screen 1 and 2 projections
b) Make a list of ideas generated during the exercise
c) Make a list of action steps
d) Write about unusual and creative images conjured up
e) Write some suggestions on how to modify the double screen exercise
f) Write stream-of-consciousness-style for a designated time period (5 or 10 minutes)

TITLE: JOURNEY AROUND THE WORLD

SUGGESTED TIME: 20 MINS

DESCRIPTION:

The exercise begins by having the imager review Target problem while comfortably sitting in workshop. Then the TP will fade-out and after a brief screen clearing, background music (source sample) will start, at which time the imager will be instructed to start a special journey around the world. The shifts in music will allow the imager to change settings. Each variation in the music should assist in creating new image projection. Prior to starting the exercise the imager should be told that certain ideas relating to TP will emerge as attention is maintained on the journey. The ideas should not be looked for, instead the imager should just let their images appear.

GUIDED INSTRUCTIONS:
— Find a comfortable position and begin focusing on your breathing
— Allow yourself now . . . to enter your workshop
— Take a moment and sense your surroundings
IMAGE SET
— Allow your TP to flow onto the screen
— Take a few moments and let the images appear
— Alright . . . clear your screen and sit back and relax
— You're going on an exciting Journey Around the World
— As the music changes let your settings change-guide yourself to a new land, a different place on Earth
— Ideas relative to your TP will emerge as you travel
— So let us begin—start music
— Alright you have finished the exercise
— Prepare to leave your workshop
— When I count to ten you will be wide awake
— One . . . ten . . . wide awake

OPTIONS:
a) Designate a certain geographical place to travel to
b) Use shorter music selection
c) Develop your own music selection to be used in exercise

d)   Don't use any music
e)   Use nature sounds: waves, crickets, forests, etc.

SUGGESTIONS FOR CPS-IMAGERY IDEA WORKBOOK
a)   Write about the different lands, countries, etc., visited
b)   Write "The most unique thing about my trip was . . ."
c)   Make a list of places visited and corresponding ideas
d)   Write a trip itinerary from your experience
e)   Create a mural

TITLE: FREE ASSOCIATION SOUNDS

SUGGESTED TIME: 5 MINS

DESCRIPTION:

In this exercise the imager will focus attention on different sounds. Each sound will be heard for approximately 15 sec. after which the imager will anticipate an idea (relative to the TP) to surface. The imager should maintain full concentration on the sound during the allowed time-letting whatever association (image or thought) emerge naturally. Repeat this procedure at least five times. Each sound production will last 15 seconds in duration followed by a brief 3 second free association period then a pause. Remember, let the sounds, images and associations flow freely and effortlessly into awareness—don't force the process.

GUIDED INSTRUCTIONS

— Find a comfortable position, relax and begin focusing on your breathing
— Allow yourself now to enter your workshop
— Take a moment and sense your surroundings
— See yourself relaxed and in your workshop
IMAGE SET
— I'm going to give you 15 sec. in which time you will focus your attention on an imaginary sound
— After the 15 second period there will be a fade-out-associate 3 second period. This will be repeated five times
— Number 1 — ready — begin 15 sec
— Fade-out-associated
— Relax 3 sec
— Numbers 2 to 5 are repeated like number 1
— Alright, you have now finished the exercise
— Prepare to leave your workshop
— When I count to ten, you will be wide awake
— One . . . ten, wide awake

OPTIONS:

a) Allow for more repetitions (10-15)
b) change the length of time given for image production, free association or relaxation pause

c) Give imager suggestions for different categories of music, e.g., country sounds, certain instrumental sounds, nature sounds, etc.
d) Repeat the same sound five times.

SUGGESTIONS FOR CPS-IMAGERY IDEA WORKBOOK
a) Describe the sounds in their order of production
b) Give a color to each sound created
c) Make a list of ideas generated during exercise

TITLE: ALTERNATE TIME-FUTURE

SUGGESTED TIME: 12 MINS

DESCRIPTION:
The imager will select certain aspects of TP which can be projected into the future. It will require the imager to select a specific component of TP and begin creating images of what it will be like in the future. There will be several opportunities for TP selection and future vision. The imager has a choice in projecting a single dimension of the TP repeatedly or selecting several dimensions for future image projection. Prior to beginning the exercise, there should be a brief discussion on the concept of future.

GUIDED INSTRUCTIONS:
— Find a comfortable position, relax, and begin focusing on your breathing
— Allow yourself now to enter your workshop
— Take a moment and sense your surroundings P = 30 sec
— See yourself sitting, comfortably in your Viewing Chair
IMAGE SET
— Begin focusing on one aspect of the TP
— Now apply future vision and see yourself as it would be in the future P = 60 sec
— Now select a different aspect of the TP
— See it in the future — just allow the images to flow onto your screen P = 30 sec
— Again, select another aspect of the TP
— Apply future vision . . . you have 30 seconds which is lots of time
— Now continue this process on your own — first select TP — then apply future vision P = 3 mins
— Alright, you have finished the exercise
— Prepare to leave your workshop
— When I count to ten, you will be back in your original setting
— One . . . ten, wide awake

OPTIONS:
a)   Be specific as to the exact future time period

b) Select only one aspect of TP
c) Have imager do the exercise non-guided
d) Use second screen for future vision projection
e) Use music with futuristic quality

SUGGESTIONS FOR CPS-IMAGERY IDEA WORKBOOK:
a) Describe how the problem was different during future vision
b) Make a list of what you learned from the experience
c) Describe other ways future vision could be used
d) Discuss why future vision is a valuable process

Bibliography

BOOKS

Ahsen, A. *Psycheye: Self-analytic Consciousness.* New York: Random House, 1977.

Bagley, M. & Hess, K. *200 Ways of Using Imagery in the Classroom.* New York: Trillium Press, 1982.

Brown. B. *Supermind.* New York: Harper & Row, Publishers, 1980.

Clark, B. *Growing Up Gifted.* Columbus, Ohio: Charles E. Merrill, 1979.

Cooper, L. & Erickson, M. *Time Distortion In Hypnosis.* Baltimore: Williams & Wilkins, 1959.

deBono, E. *Laterial Thinking.* New York: Basic Books, 1970.

Edwards, B. *Drawing On The Right Side Of The Brain.* Los Angeles, Calif: J. P. Tarcher, Inc., 1979.

Emerson, R. W. "Conduct Of Life: Beauty" *The Complete Works of Ralph Waldo Emerson.* Boston: Houghton Mifflin, 1903.

Ferguson, M. *The Acquarian Conspiracy.* Los Angeles, Calif.: J. P. Tarcher, Inc., 1980.

Garfield, P. *Creative Dreaming.* New York: Simon & Schuster, 1974.

Green, E. & Green, A. *Beyond Biofeedback.* New York: Delacorte, 1977.

Houston, J. *The Possible Human.* Los Angeles, Calif.: J. P. Tarcher, Inc. 1982.

Hutchinson, E. *How To Think Creatively.* New York: Abingdon-Cokesbury, 1949.

Ironson, D. Human High Technology: Part 1. *Journal of Creative Thinking,* Vol. 6, 178-180, 1982.

James, W. *Great Men, Great Thoughts, & The Environment.* Atlantic Monthly, 1880, 46, 441-459.

Laing, R. D. *Politics of Experience.* New York: Pantheon Books, 1967.

Lozanov, G. The Nature & History of the Suggestopedia System of Teaching Foreign Language & Its Experimental Prospects. *Suggestology & Suggestopedia Journal,* Vol. 1, No. 1, 1975.

Mackinnon, D. Creativity and Transliminal Experience. *Journal of Creative Behavior,* 1971, 5 (4), 227-241.

Maslow, A. *Toward A Psychology of Being.* New York: Van Nostrand, 1968.

McKim, R. *Experience In Visual Thinking.* Belmount, Calif: Wadsworth, 1972.

Murphy, J. *The Power of Your Subconscious Mind.* Englewood Cliffs, NJ: Prentice Hall, Inc., 1963.

Ostrander, S. & Schroderer, L. *Super Learning.* New York. Dell Publishing Co. Inc. 1979.

Parnes, S. et al. *Guide To Creative Action.* New York: Scribner, 1977.

Peale, N. V. *Positive Imaging.* New York: Fawcett Crest Books, 1979.

Penfield, W. The Brain's Record of Auditory and Visual Experience—A Final Summary & Discussion, *Brain*, 1963, 86, 595-696.

Progogine, I. *From Being To Becoming.* San Francisco: Freeman, 1980.

Richardson, A. *Mental Imagery.* New York: Springer, 1969.

Rogers, C. *On Becoming A Person.* Houghton Mifflin Co. Boston: 1961.

Rugg, H. *Imagination.* New York: Harper & Row, Publishers, 1963.

Sagan, C. *The Dragons Of Eden.* New York: Random House. 1977.

Samuels, M. & Samuels, N. *Seeing With The Mind's Eye.* New York: Random House, 1975.

Suchman, J. R. *Developing Inquiry Skills.* Ill. SRA. 1970.

Torrance, E. P. *Education of the Creative Potential.* Minneapolis: Univ. of Minn. Press. 1963.

Walkup, L. Detecting Creativity: Some Practical Approaches. *Journal of Creative Behavior*, 1971, 5 (2), 88-93.

NEW AGE MUSIC:

The Angels of Comfort/Angel Play. Sausalito, CA: Inter-Dimensional Music.
Bamboo Waterfall. Pacific Grove, CA: Tape Masters.
Spectrum Suite—Extended Play. Belmont, CA: Halpern Sounds.
Music for an Inner Journey. Carmel, CA: Steve Berman.
A Thousand Moods. Milwaukee, WI: Sona Gala Productions.
Golden Voyage. Culver City, CA: Awakening Productions.
Source Sampler, Vol. 1. Pacific Grove, CA: Source Music.
The Atlantis Healing Harp. Malibu, CA: Valley of the Sun Publishing.

BAROQUE MUSIC:

Largo from "Winter" from the Four Seasons (Vivaldi, A.).
Aria (or Sarabande) to the Goldberg Variations, BWV 988 (Bach).
Largo from Harpsichord Concerto in F Minor, BWV 1056 (Bach).
Largo from Concerto No. 1 in F (Brass) from Music for the Royal Fireworks. (Handel).
Largo from Concerto in G Major for Viola and String Orchestra (Teleman).

IMAGERY NOTES

IMAGERY NOTES